Effective
Television Advertising

About MSI

Founded in 1961, the Marketing Science Institute (MSI) is a nonprofit center for research in marketing. Supported by major corporations for the purpose of advancing marketing practice and knowledge, the Institute brings together the interests and resources of industry and academia to address issues of key importance to marketing. Individual topic areas are identified for study by the Institute's Board of Trustees, representing member companies and the academic community.

Member companies reflect the marketing activities and research needs of a wide variety of consumer and industrial product and service businesses. MSI's academic relationships are also broadly based. Leading researchers from many schools are involved in MSI research. Normally, some 25 to 30 schools may be represented at any given time among the researchers who are engaged in some aspect of MSI research.

The Institute conducts research and disseminates research results to the business and academic communities through its workshops, conferences, mini-conferences, and steering group meetings as well as through its publication series. The Institute also issues a Newsletter and Research Briefs that call attention to projects and research findings of interest.

The Marketing Science Institute's primary source of financial support comes from the 40 individual companies that are members of the Institute. The Institute also receives funding through grants from government agencies, foundations, and associations.

Effective Television Advertising is the first book in a series to be published jointly by MSI and Lexington Books.

Effective Television Advertising

A *Study of 1000 Commercials*

David W. Stewart
Owen Graduate School of Management
Vanderbilt University

David H. Furse
Nashville Consulting Group

Lexington Books
D.C. Heath and Company/Lexington, Massachusetts/Toronto

Library of Congress Cataloging-in-Publication Data

Stewart, David W.
   Effective television advertising.

   Bibliography: p.
   Includes index.
   1. Television advertising.   I.   Furse, David H.
II.   Title.
HF6146.T42S845   1986   659.14'3   85-45448
ISBN 0-669-11751-X (alk. paper)

Published simultaneously in Canada
Printed in the United States of America
International Standard Book Number: 0-669-11751-X
Library of Congress Catalog Card Number: 85-45448

The paper used in this publication meets the minimum requirements of
American National Standard for Information Sciences—Permanence of
Paper for Printed Library Materials, ANSI Z3.48-1984.

Contents

Foreword

Alden G. Clayton, President
Marketing Science Institute

P ublication of *Effective Television Advertising: A Study of 1000 Commercials* is a landmark event in several ways. The magnitude of the data base is most unusual. An exceptional amount of variance within the data pool provided rich information for analysis. One thousand fifty-nine television commercials reflected viewer response to 356 brands, among 12 product categories; advertising for 63 firms was represented. The range of response, as measured in the testing procedure, was exceptionally broad. Related recall scores ranged from 5 percent to 80 percent, key message comprehension ranged from 0 percent to 68 percent, and persuasion ranged from − 7 percent to 54 percent. In contrast to testing systems which use a single benchmark of effectiveness, the multiple measures available for this study provided the basis for a powerful analysis.

Finally, this book was made possible only through a rare collaboration among the four constituencies which form the advertising research community—advertisers, advertising agencies, research firms, and academics. Research Systems Corporation (RSC) contributed the base of commercial tests and helped in organizing the enormous task of coding them for analysis. (About two thousand hours were devoted to this phase of the study). Advertisers and advertising agencies, working through the Advertising Research Steering Group of the Marketing Science Institute, initially encouraged the study and then furnished advice and counsel to the researchers at all stages of the project. A group of sponsors provided funding for the research. Scholarship was, of course, provided by David W. Stewart and David H. Furse, who were colleagues on the Vanderbilt faculty when the study started.

The completed project and this subsequent book serve as an excellent example of how, by working together, results can be achieved that could not be accomplished by working alone. As such, *Effective Television Advertising* is a model for marketing research, and we are gratified to have helped make it possible.

Preface

The study reported in this book was conceived in early 1981 and completed in late 1984. It was conceived out of a sense that too little was known about broadcast advertising and that a large-scale descriptive study was needed to identify directions for future research. It was also conceived out of a sense of frustration with much of what has recently been published as advertising research. Shanteau (1983, p. 160) suggested that "the reason for studying advertising is to answer questions about advertising, not about cognitive processes." It seemed to us that much of the contemporary work on advertising was concerned less with advertising than with other phenomena. It appeared only incidental that advertising was the stimulus material used in such research.

Much of contemporary advertising research has severe limitations. No convincing theory of advertising has emerged to guide research in the field. Theories have been borrowed from other fields, but little in these borrowed theories suggests precise, testable hypotheses. It appeared to us that a large, well-executed, descriptive study could be a useful contribution to the literature and the progress of theory development. It was our hope that such a study would suggest new avenues for research and provide a better insight into how advertising is different from other types of communication.

We have been particularly concerned by the use of ad hoc measures of effectiveness in much of the research on persuasive communication. Academic studies, on the one hand, have concentrated on the development of theory but have lagged in the development of reliable and valid measures of marketing effectiveness. On the other hand, industry researchers have been concerned less with the development of general theories than with more reliable and valid measures of advertising effectiveness. Measurement and theory must be brought together in a single study if progress is to be made.

Our study began with a search for a defensible set of measures of advertising effectiveness. We believe the primary measure of concern for advertising research should be consumer choice, a measure usually ignored in published research. We expect many academic researchers will be uncomfortable with our study; it represents a departure from the major paradigms of research in the field. We believe these paradigms neither have been very helpful to managers nor have they advanced our understanding of advertising. We suggest the need for a new paradigm for research in our concluding chapter, a paradigm that emphasizes choice behavior and the use of reliable and valid measures.

A study of the size and breadth of the one reported here is not the result of the efforts of just two researchers. The project represents the cooperative efforts of a large number of individuals and organizations. We are particularly grateful to the Marketing Science Institute (MSI) for the primary financial support of the project. Representatives of the corporate sponsors within MSI also provided valuable input throughout the study. This input included suggestions of factors to be examined in the study and types of analyses. We owe a special debt of gratitude to Diane Schmalensee, director of research operations at MSI, who coordinated the flow of information between the researchers and the sponsoring organizations.

Research Systems Corporation of Evansville, Indiana, was a full partner in the research reported in this book. Research Systems Corporation was identified as having an appropriate set of advertising performance measures for the study after a systematic review of the major advertising copy-testing services was conducted in 1980. The firm has cooperated beyond our highest expectations. Research Systems Corporation has provided access to a large set of television commercials for descriptive coding, data on the copy-test performance of those commercials, and assistance in coding over 1,000 commercials, data processing, and data interpretation. Two members of the Research Systems Corporation staff deserve particular mention and an expression of gratitude. Meg Blair, president, offered insightful comments and helpful ideas throughout the study. Her experience with advertising copy testing and the specific measures employed by her company was an important resource. Allan Kuse, manager of basic research, was our on-site coordinator for the study. His contribution was substantial, and we regard him as a third author of the book.

We also owe a note of appreciation to the numerous graduate students at the Owen Graduate School of Management, Vanderbilt University, who assisted us with the study. Connie Pechmann deserves a particular word of thanks for her work on code development and data analysis. Maureen Writesman bore the burden of typing and retyping the manuscript, and we thank her for her patience and good humor. The Owen Graduate School of Management, through the Dean's Fund for Faculty Research, and the Nashville Consulting Group, Inc., provided additional financial support for the study.

Finally, we owe a large debt to our families. A 4-year study involving much travel, late night data analysis, and weekend writing took precious time from our families. It is to our families that we dedicate this work: Gunn, Kristina, and Erik Furse and Lenora, Sarah, and Rachel Stewart.

1
Introduction

The creation and production of effective advertising has long been a concern of both advertisers and advertising agencies. Various rules of thumb for creating effective advertisements have existed since advertising began. Systematic research on the creation of effective advertising dates from the turn of the century. A substantial body of knowledge concerning the effects of different executional devices on the recall of print advertising developed during the first third of the twentieth century. Research by psychologists Walter Dill Scott (1903, 1908a and b), Edward K. Strong (1912, 1916), and Daniel Starch (1923), as well as work by marketing and advertising practitioners such as Percival White (1927) and John Caples (1933), examined the effects of type of appeal, color, illustration, layout, and copy treatment. The results of this work suggested that a sizeable proportion of the observed variation in the recognition and recall of print advertisements could be accounted for by simple mechanical factors.

More recent research on print advertising appears to verify earlier conclusions. Twedt (1952) regressed the readership scores of 137 print advertisements appearing in *The American Builder* on a large number of variables and found that the size of the advertisement, size of the illustration, and number of colors accounted for 50 percent of the variance in readership. Diamond (1968) used six Starch readership scores as the dependent variables in an analysis of 1,070 advertisements in *Life*. Diamond found that the Starch score was higher the larger the advertisement, the greater the number of colors, the fewer the number of advertisements in the issue, if the ad were on the right-hand page, and if it had a photograph rather than an illustration. Diamond validated his findings by predicting the Starch scores of an independent sample of 43 advertisements in a later issue, and his equations had coefficients of determination as high as .74.

Assael, Kofron, and Burg (1967) and Valiente (1973) also reported that mechanical factors accounted for substantial variance in advertising recognition scores. Holbrook and Lehmann (1980) developed an elaborate coding system for both message content and mechanical factors in print advertising.

They found that mechanical factors accounted for 10 to 13 percent of the variance in ad recognition scores, while message content accounted for 17 to 21 percent of the variance in such measures. Rossiter (1981) criticized this study on methodological grounds and suggested an alternative coding system consisting of thirteen executional variables (visual and psycholinguistic) that accounted for over 40 percent of the variance in advertising recognition scores without consideration of message content.

Hendon (1973) reviewed 50 years of research on the influence of mechanical factors on print advertising performance. He concluded that where the content of competing advertising is similar, the mechanical or graphic elements in the message are the only tools available for making the advertising memorable. Percy (1983) has provided a more recent review of the influence of specific executional factors on the performance of print advertising.

While much is known about the influence of mechanical and content factors on the performance of print advertising, far less is known about broadcast advertising. No major studies comparable to those for print advertising have been carried out for broadcast ads (Kotler and Lilien 1983). It is also unclear whether or not findings of research involving print advertising are generalizable to broadcast advertising. Television not only changes the nature of executional variables but also greatly expands their number by adding sound and motion and the nuances of their combined effects on advertising performance. The viewer comes to the broadcast medium in a more passive state than the reader of print media. While reading is, by definition, a cognitive activity, it is less clear that viewing a television commercial within the typical viewing environment produces cognitive responses. Wright (1981) offers evidence that thought outputs may approach zero for broadcast ads and suggests that the rather substantial clutter of the broadcast medium environment may actually suppress cognitive response. Broadcast ads also do not provide the opportunity for audience self-pacing of exposure to the commercial message, while print ads do.

Research on print advertising has tended to concentrate on recognition or recall as the sole measures of advertising effectiveness. There has been a growing concern that recall is not a sufficient basis for evaluating advertising effectiveness (see, for example, Gibson 1983; Ross 1982; Zielske 1982). It is not clear that the same factors that influence the recall or recognition of an advertisement also influence its persuasiveness.

The academic literature has few studies of the impact of executional variables on television advertising performance. Those that have been published have focused on a single or, at most, relatively few message executional factors. Several industry studies have been more comprehensive but suffer other problems. Ramond (1976) reviewed the limited and often contradictory available research on television advertising and drew the following conclusions:

1. Shorter television commercials are recalled equally as well as longer ones.
2. Sex, humor, and fear have no consistent effect on what advertising communicates.
3. Awareness and attitude change are sensitive to differences in television commercial execution and can predict changes in brand choices.
4. Product class has a significant effect on recognition and recall measures.
5. Ads need not be believed to be remembered.
6. Because television commercials vary in more ways than print ads and have been studied for a shorter time, less is known about the effects of specific executional variables.

There exists a need for a large-sample, comprehensive study of broadcast advertising. That study should examine the impact of executional and general message factors on several measures of advertising performance. This book was designed to fill this gap in the advertising knowledge base.

Purpose and Philosophy of the Study

This study sought answers to four general questions:

1. How much variance in advertising performance is attributable to executional variables (individually, as subsets, and in total)?
2. Where is the impact of a particular executional variable (or subset of such variables) manifest? In recall measures? Persuasion measures? Both recall and persuasion?
3. Are there differences in executional effects across market situations (for example, product category, stage in the product life cycle, brand loyalty)? Do executional factors appear to manifest significant effects in one subset of commercials but not in others?
4. What relationships exist among various measures of advertising performance?

The study was designed to add to the descriptive literature on the effects of various advertising executional devices on measures of advertising performance. The focus of the study was broadcast advertising—specifically, television commercials. It was particularly concerned with three outcome measures: related recall, key message comprehension, and persuasion (measured as a shift in brand choice). The study was designed to examine the influence of television advertising execution on representative sets of consumers viewing commercials within a fairly typical exposure setting. The commercial was the unit of analysis rather than the individual respondents. The commercials employed were actual commercials produced by advertising agencies for advertisers.

Research of the type reported in this study is characterized as *effects* research (Calder, Phillips, and Tybout 1981) or *preparatory* research (McGrath and Brinberg 1983). Prior research of this type has suffered severe limitations because it has involved small laboratory tests of mock ads in non-typical settings using nonrepresentative samples (Shimp and Gresham 1983). While such research may be appropriate for testing specific theoretical hypotheses, it is inappropriate for examining the impact of advertising factors for practical applications or for establishing the external validity of observed effects. The more common problems with prior effects research are described in the following:

1. *The unit of analysis has usually been the individual rather than the commercial.* Management decisions require decisions about commercials and must be made on the basis of the general, aggregate response of the target audience. The effects of individual differences on responses to commercials is useful information to managers only insofar as these differences may form a basis for defining market subsegments. Most individual differences that have been shown to interact with executional variables are inappropriate for audience segmentation. The most appropriate unit of analysis is the commercial, with individual respondents in the defined target audience considered as replications.

2. *A single measure of advertising effectiveness has typically been employed rather than a pattern of responses on multiple measures.* It is not apparent what measure of advertising effectiveness is the most appropriate under given circumstances. Recall measures, persuasion measures, attitudinal measures, and physiological measures are currently used by copytesting organizations. Much of the research on executional variables has been carried out using a single indicator of advertising effect. It is probably reasonable to hypothesize that different executional variables will manifest their effects in different measures. Executional variables that influence recall measures may not influence persuasion, and vice versa. Independent research focusing on the same executional variable may reach different conclusions only because of differences in dependent measures.

3. *Measures of advertising effectiveness have often lacked demonstrated reliability and validity.* A demonstration of measure reliability and validity should precede the use of any dependent measure of advertising performance. Otherwise it is impossible to determine whether the changes in the dependent measures are the result of measurement error (in the case

of an unrealiable measure) and whether the change actually represents the market response that it is assumed to represent (validity of the measure). Much of the prior research in the field has employed ad hoc measures with assumed rather than demonstrated reliability and validity.

4. *Rather small numbers of commercials have been employed in the majority of previous studies.* In many cases, as few as two commercial executions have been used as the basis for inferring general executional effects. The representativeness of such small numbers of executions is impossible to determine. This is a particularly severe problem if product category and/or brand effects interact with executional variables to produce changes in measures of advertising effect, which they undoubtedly do. Since most prior research on executional variables has focused on a single executional variable (or very small subset of such variables), interactions among executional variables have seldom been examined. When interaction effects have been examined, they have usually been found to be statistically significant.

5. *Research has frequently employed relatively small convenience samples.* Samples of 20 to 40 respondents are common. Small samples, combined with low reliability of measures, tend to produce a weak and insensitive test of the effects of executional variables. College sophomores and MBA students have frequently been the populations from which test samples have been selected. Well-designed and controlled samplings of targeted consumer groups have been the exception rather than the rule in published research to date.

Ray (1975) has suggested that the development of a theory of advertising must be based on empirical observations involving several different measures, controlled field experiments with a representative sampling of conditions (products, appeals, formats), and controls that minimize reactivity and test effects. In addition, measures and models employed in developing such a theory must be validated. Little of the research to date has measured up to these standards. The present research attempted to address the limitations of prior research in the following ways:

1. It identifies a larger set of executional variables than has previously been employed and examines the reliability of the variables prior to further analysis.

2. It employs multiple reliable and valid measures of advertising performance.

3. It employs data generated from large samples that are representative of the audiences for whom the advertisements were intended.

4. It controls for differential effects of product category and life cycle.
5. It examines relationships among executional variables individually and in combination and among measures of advertising performance.
6. It employs a large and diverse sample of television commercials.

Outline of the Research

Much of the presentation of the study is necessarily detailed and technical. Sufficient information is provided for interested researchers to replicate the results of the study, and the sheer magnitude and complexity of the dataset add to the complexity of detail. To aid the reader in understanding the organization of the research report and to facilitate the identification of those portions of the study most relevant for different readers' interests, a brief outline of the format is offered.

Chapter 2 provides a discussion of the conceptual and theoretical bases for the study, a review of prior research most directly relevant to the present study, and an overview of the findings of the study. For the reader interested only in the conclusions of the study, chapters 2 and 8 will be sufficient. Details of the procedures and analyses used in the study are provided in chapters 3 through 7.

Chapter 3 describes the development of the coding system for the message executional variables examined in the study. It discusses how executional variables were identified, the reliability checks on these variables, and some of the problems encountered in designing a coding system. Executional variables that were intended for inclusion but that could not be coded for reliability are also described. The selection and coding of commercials in the database are also described in chapter 3.

Chapter 4 is concerned with the measures of advertising performance employed in the study. It describes the copy-testing methodology employed by Research Systems Corporation and describes the three measures of advertising performance used in the study: (1) related recall, (2) key message comprehension, and (3) persuasion. The chapter provides evidence of the reliability and validity of the measures, as well as a discussion of the limitations of the measures. Product category and brand factors that influence the persuasion measure are discussed as well as the procedures employed in the present study for eliminating the confounding effects of product category from the more general findings relating advertising execution and measures of advertising performance. The chapter closes with a discussion of the relationships among the measures.

Chapter 5 provides a discussion of the simple univariate and bivariate relationships obtained from the data. The reliability of individual executional items is reported, along with the frequency of occurrence of individual items. The chapter provides a descriptive overview of the dataset, but caution should be exercised when drawing conclusions based on simple bivariate relationships. Some individual executional variables do not occur with sufficient frequency to separate their effect clearly from product category effects. Also, simple bivariate relationships may disguise more complex relationships, or interaction effects, in which related sets of executional variables are causing the observed effect on advertising performance.

Chapter 6 moves beyond simple bivariate relationships and tries to capture the greater complexity and richness of the dataset. The results of a factor analysis of the executional items are reported. The factors are related to the commercial performance measures.

Chapter 7 is concerned with the influence of specific moderators on the relationships between advertising execution and measures of performance. These moderators are product life cycle (new/improved versus more established products), degree of switching in the product category, brand market share (for example, pre-exposure brand choice), number of competing brands, and form of the test commercial (finished versus storyboard).

Chapter 8 discusses the findings of the study, draws some general conclusions concerning television advertising, and offers suggestions for future research. It also discusses the limitations in the study and raises the need for caution when interpreting the present findings.

2
Background and Overview

A descriptive study of the type reported here would be far less important, although still interesting, if a strong theory of advertising existed. Such a theory would suggest those factors that are and are not important for influencing the viewer of a television commercial. It would serve to focus studies on a particular subset of factors that influence one or more measures of viewer response to advertising and would suggest the nature of the relationships to be expected among variables. A strong theory would specify the form of measurement of the various factors to be examined and would suggest the situations or circumstances where expected relationships would hold. Unfortunately, no such theory exists for advertising. As late as 1975, Ray suggested that the field of behavioral research in advertising was not ready for theory development, at least not in the sense of a strong, formal, positive network of facts about consumer response. Although much research and conceptualizing has occurred since Ray's paper, the basic situation has not changed. More recently, Shanteau (1983), commenting on several reviews of information-processing approaches to the study of advertising, concluded, "what are generally viewed as theories in the advertising/consumer research area are not really theories at all" (p. 161). The two most prevalent conceptualizations of advertising effects both fall considerably short as theories of advertising. One is an old standby, the hierarchy-of-effects model; the other is of somewhat more recent origin, the cognitive response model.

The hierarchy-of-effects model was introduced to the marketing literature by Lavidge and Steiner (1961). These models can be traced to earlier work on the psychology of persuasion (Hovland, Janis, and Kelley 1953; Sherif and Cantril 1945, 1946; Strong 1925). Since the introduction of the original model, numerous variations and elaborations have been suggested. Moriarty (1983) provides a brief but useful comparison of ten variations on the hierarchy model. These models suggest successive stages of the effects of persuasive communication: (1) the message gains *attention*, (2) holds *interest*, (3) arouses a *desire*, and (4) prompts *action*. Ray (1973) has suggested that the order of these effects may vary from consumer to consumer and from product class to product class.

Research on the hierarchy-of-effects model has provided mixed support for the theory. While much research suggests that the stages suggested by the model do exist and occur in the specified order, other research has failed to find support for the hierarchy (Palda 1966). Moriarty (1983) has criticized hierarchy-of-effects models for conceptualizing the effects of persuasive communication in a lock-step hierarchical form rather than recognizing the inter-relationships of effects. She argues these effects often occur simultaneously, not in a particular sequence. While the hierarchy-of-effects model remains useful for conceptualizing the effects of persuasive communication, it appears to be too simplistic to explain fully the influence of those communications on cognition and behavior. Indeed, hierarchy of effects is less a theory than a conceptual framework for thinking about relationships. No accepted opera-tionalization of the model exists in the form of demonstrably reliable and valid measures.

The cognitive response approach, as originally outlined by Greenwald (1968), suggests that when people receive persuasive communications they will attempt to relate the new information to their existing knowledge about the topic. The receiver will generate cognitions, responses that mediate the relationship between the communication and other responses. This approach has generated substantial research and has become the dominant research paradigm for investigating the effects of persuasive communications. Petty, Ostrom, and Brock (1981) summarize much of the basic research on cogni-tive response. Examples of the application of this approach to marketing and advertising problems are found in Wright (1973), Petty (1977a), Calder and Sternthal (1980), and Olson, Toy, and Dover (1982). There seems to be little question that cognitive responses, when they occur, may mediate the rela-tionship between a persuasive communication and other responses. The approach is not without its critics, however.

Lutz and Swasy (1977), for example, have criticized cognitive response models on measurement grounds. Most operational measures of cognitive response have been developed on an intuitive, ad hoc basis. Controversy persists about the most appropriate types of measures to employ. Calder and Sternthal (1980) attributed their failure to obtain support for the mediational role of cognitive responses to differences in measures used to assess cognitive response. Anderson (1981) has raised other problems with the cognitive response model, including the presence of biases in self-report data such as the halo effect, the inappropriate use of correlational designs, and problems associated with the use of thought-listing procedures, which are ambiguous about causal direction. Consistent with this latter criticism is a study by Belch (1981) that found no differences in various outcome measures associated with comparative versus noncomparative advertising but that did find differ-ences in cognitive responses.

The most damaging criticism of the application of cognitive response theory to advertising has come from Wright (1981). He argues that much of the research on cognitive response has been carried out in settings that encourage thinking. High-involvement topics are presented to reasonably motivated, bright, thinking individuals (typically college students) who are instructed in advance that thoughts about the communication will be of interest. In addition, rather long periods of exposure to stimulus material have been provided. Such situations, by design, produce cognitive responses. Wright questions whether such situations are typical of the viewing situations of heterogeneous audiences reacting to audiovisual advertising when not hypermotivated. In fact, Wright suggests that cognitive responses may not even occur in the typical broadcast advertising exposure situation. Thus, cognitive response theory, while perhaps useful for explaining behavior in a highly structured laboratory situation, does not appear to offer a currently acceptable basis for understanding response to broadcast advertising. Further, there remains the problem of a well-accepted operationalization of the theory.

Fishbein and Ajzen, after reviewing much of the literature on cognitive processes in persuasion, conclude:

> We are convinced that the persuasiveness of a communication can be increased much more easily and dramatically by paying careful attention to its content than by manipulation of credibility, attractiveness, fear, self-esteem, distraction, or any of the other myriad factors that have caught the fancy of investigators in the area of communication and persuasion. [1981, p. 359]

Indeed, these authors express concern that many of the effects attributable to nonmessage factors (for example, type of appeal, source) may occur as a result of differential information content, not the nonmessage factor per se. Thus, cognitive response models may not even be able to specify a clear relationship between the causal stimulus and the cognitive response, assuming that a cognitive response has occurred at all.

Both the cognitive response model and the hierarchy-of-effects models offer some assistance in designing a study of advertising effects, but neither satisfies the conditions to qualify as a theory of advertising. Neither offers a set of well-defined measures, a comprehensive statement of what effects are important, or a set of unambiguous and testable propositions about specific relationships. Both sets of models are better for explaining events than predicting events. Research involving these models has been criticized for ignoring choice behavior as an important variable, concentrating instead on attitude and intention (Shanteau 1983). Choice behavior is the ultimate criterion against which the performance of most advertising must be evaluated.

In the absense of a well-defined theory, it is necessary to look to the practitioner for help. Indeed, to the extent that a practitioner, an advertiser or advertising agency, has a well-defined advertising philosophy, that philosophy may be regarded as a theory of advertising. More than 40 years ago, Rosser Reeves espoused a creative philosophy for advertising that called for each product to develop its own unique selling proposition (USP) and to use whatever devices and repetition were necessary to communicate that proposition (Higgens 1965). Borden (1942), perhaps the most important academic advertising researcher of the past 50 years, suggested much the same principle: Effective advertising provides a basis for differentiating products. Ogilvy (1964) also argued for the importance of differentiating products. In the case of Ogilvy, this differentiating was done by creating a unique product image rather than a tangible product benefit. This was largely the result of Ogilvy's work with products such as perfumes, cigarettes, and liquor that did not materially differ from one another along tangible dimensions. The principle is the same, however. Advertising should differentiate the product from its competitors if it is to be memorable and persuasive. Thus, brand differentiation is one executional factor that practitioners regard as important for persuasive advertising. Other executional and message factors of import to advertising practitioners may be found in published studies and are reviewed in the following section.

Industry Studies of Television Advertising Execution

At least four earlier efforts have explored the impact of television advertising execution on a large scale. These efforts have been made by industry researchers; only one of these studies has been published in a widely disseminated journal, a study carried out by Leo Burnett's Creative Research Workshop and reported by McEwen and Leavitt (1976).

The purpose of the McEwen and Leavitt (1976) study was to find a relatively few natural groupings of executional elements that accounted for an appreciable amount of the variability among commercials and to relate these groupings to advertising recall. The study began with 293 specific executional items (for example, contains music, has a visible announcer) that had been identified as important by experts in the advertising creative and research fields. Five judges were asked to view 100 commercials for inexpensive, frequently purchased consumer products and asked to check each of the 293 items for the commercial as "yes," "no," or "irrelevant/does not apply." Items demonstrating low interrater reliability or those that appeared to apply to almost all commercials were eliminated, leaving 250 individual items. These 250 items were then related to recall measures, and an aggregate discrimination score was developed for differentiating high-recall commercials from low-recall commercials.

Further analysis reduced the 250 items to 90 items after eliminating redundant items and items that failed to discriminate significantly between high and low recall. The 90 executional variables were used by a second group of judges to evaluate the original pool of 100 commercials. This second phase involved a five-interval applicability scale (ranging from "definitely describes this commercial" to "doesn't describe it at all" rather than a simple "yes/no" choice. A factor analysis of these 90 items produced 12 independent factors (table 2–1) that accounted for 61 percent of the total variance in commercial execution.

Table 2–1
Key Element Factors from the McEwen and Leavitt Study

Factor	Item	Loading
Empathic product integration	The setting has people in it.	.78
	It shows people like my friends and neighbors.	.68
	The main character is clear.	.63
	The commercial shows product users.	.60
	The relationship between characters is close.	.54
	The people participate in some action together.	.53
Integrated announcer	A testimonial figure holds/tastes the product.	.83
	There is a visible announcer.	.76
	A celebrity demonstrates the product.	.63
	The commercial looks like an interview.	.57
	The commercial uses voice-over.	− .66
Demonstration	The commercial has a demonstration.	.91
	The demonstration shows a consumer benefit.	.84
	The demonstration shows people seen elsewhere.	.75
Pleasant liveliness	It is a generally active commercial.	.65
	The commercial uses dissolves or fades.	− .64
	The commercial has music in it.	.64
	It shows children or babies.	.59
	It looks like a variety or musical show.	.58
Confusion	The commerical follows an orderly sequence.	− .69
	It uses unusual photographic techniques.	.63
	It has more than five settings/situations.	.63
	The commercial seems cluttered.	.52
New product introduction	The commercial is for an old, established brand.	− .74
	The commercial is for a new product.	.66
	The commerical shows mothers.	.64
Structured product story	The relationship between the characters is concerned with the product.	.66
	The commercial builds to a climax.	.49
	The commercial seems to have a beginning, middle, and end.	.44

Table 2–1 (continued)

Factor	Item	Loading
Problem solution	There is a problem solution in the commercial.	.77
	The problem is solved by people.	.74
	The problem solution takes place in an ordinary setting.	.73
	The characters say something I had heard someone else say before.	.52
Animation	The cartoon figure used is instantly recognizable.	.80
	There is a cartoon or animated figure used.	.80
Unpleasant stimulation	The color seems irritating or bothersome.	.78
	There is a demonstration using charts or graphs.	.63
	It looks like a news documentary.	.61
	The commercial emphasizes red shades.	.53
	It has a surprise ending.	.43
Persuasive stimulation	It makes you feel that you could practically touch or smell or taste or feel the product.	.73
	It makes you think of the times you used the product.	.66
	It makes you want to buy the product.	.60
	The commercial is in color.	.55
	The music is distinctive.	.55
Opening	The opening makes me think it was for another product.	.67
	The commercial depends on suspense or surprise.	.51
	The lead-in is directly related to the product.	− .62
	The commercial has a minimum of sound.	.43

Source: J. McEwen and C. Leavitt, 1976, "A Way to Describe TV Commercials," *Journal of Advertising Research,* 16:35–39.

Four of the twelve factors appeared to be consistently related to recall:

Demonstration by people (positively related to recall),

Structured product story (positively related to recall),

Confusion (negatively related to recall),

Opening suspense (negatively related to recall).

The remaining eight factors did not appear to affect recall consistently. However, use of product users or announcers with the product presentation was related but less consistently.

An important implication of the McEwen and Leavitt study was that a finite number of executional elements in commercials could be identified, reliably coded, and related to a measure of advertising effectiveness. The study suggests some of the important executional variables that should be incorporated into future studies. It does suffer, however, from the following limitations: (1) recall was the only measure of advertising effectiveness; (2) the commercial base, although far larger than for many studies, was still rather small; and (3) reliability and validity of the recall measure used had not been demonstrated.

More recently, a proprietary study carried out by Mapes and Ross, a firm which provides commercial copytesting services, and briefly reported by Ogilvy and Raphaelson (1982) examined the relationships between certain executional variables and two measures of advertising effectiveness—recall and a measure of change in brand preference indexed by product category norms (Moore 1982). The study involved 809 commercials for food products, appliances, apparel, and five other unspecified product categories. Television commercials that scored above average in ability to change brand preference had the following executional characteristics:

> Problem/solution format,
>
> Humor pertinent to selling proposition,
>
> Advertising-developed characters or personalities who become associated with a brand,
>
> Slice-of-life enactments where a doubter is converted,
>
> Newness (new product, new uses, new ideas, new information),
>
> Candid camera testimonials,
>
> Demonstrations.

Commercials built around celebrities were not notably successful in changing brand preference but did appear to increase the level of recall. Other findings of the study suggested the following:

1. Cartoons and animation are effective with children but below average with adults.

2. Commercials with a lot of very short scenes and many changes of situation are below average.

3. Supers (words on the screen) add to the advertisement's power to change brand preference if the words reinforce the main point.

4. Commercials that do not show the package or that end without giving the brand name are below average in changing brand preference.

5. Commercials that start with the key idea stand a better chance of holding and persuading the viewer.

6. Character actor rather than bland stereotype performances are above average in ability to change brand preferences.

7. Visual devices (mnemonics) increase brand identification when repeated over a long period.

The findings summarized by Ogilvy and Raphaelson (1982) are characterized as applying primarily to advertising in which appeal to reason is an important element. Factors related to emotional persuasion were not reported in this analysis.

In spite of the published summary by Ogilvy and Raphaelson (1982), Mapes and Ross regards the study as proprietary, and it is available for a fee only to clients of the organization (Moore 1982). Since details of the study are not public, it is difficult to evaluate its technical soundness and the validity of its conclusions. This was not the first proprietary study, however. Other proprietary studies have been reported by McCollum/Spielman (1976), Radio Recall Research (1981), and Burke Marketing Research (1978).

The study by Radio Recall Research (1981) focused on memorability of radio commercials. Among the factors reported to affect proven recall of radio commercials were:

Number of words,

Number of brand mentions,

Number of ideas,

Story format (as opposed to straight announcement or sing-and-sell).

Neither humor nor music was reported to affect recall systematically, and sex of spokesperson appeared to have little impact in the Radio Recall Research study.

The Burke (1978) study investigated the effects of executional variables on recall of television commercials. Sixteen executional variables were examined:

Commercial length,

Early brand identification,

Brand repetition in audio,

Brand repetition in video,

Commercial format (presenter/slice of life),

Presence of celebrity,

Race of actors,

Presence of testimonials,

Use of product demonstration,

Use of animation,

moderated by whether the product being advertised is new or established or has a high or low market share. Further, the effects of executional devices on measures of comprehension and persuasion may be moderated by the level of recall created by the commercial. These interaction effects have not been examined in previous research. When measures of advertising effectiveness are correlated, it is important to examine not only the relationships between individual executional factors and an individual measure but also how an executional factor is related to shared sources of variation among measures.

7. No general conclusions regarding any executional variable can be drawn from these studies since they used different measures of performance, examined different executional factors, and employed different analytic procedures.

Nevertheless, these industry studies do provide a basis for identifying a large set of television advertising executional devices that practitioners believe may influence the performance of a television commercial.

Each of these investigations of the effects of execution on television advertising performance provides a portion of the foundation of the present study. These studies, along with direct input from practitioners, review of the academic literature, and direct observation of television commercials, provided the basis for the identification of the executional factors examined in the present study. The study was designed under the assumption that advertising remains in a pretheoretic stage of development. According to Kuhn (1970), this stage in the development of a science requires the assemblage of facts and observations, simple classificatory endeavors, and the discovery of empirical relationships. Only later, after much empirical data are available, is theory a realistic possibility.

The present study was designed to uncover relationships among demonstrably reliable sets of measures. The research is a field study; therefore, inferences of causality must be made with care. Relationships of the present findings and those of other studies are pointed out as appropriate, and some speculative explanations for the present findings are offered. These should be regarded as hypotheses for future testing rather than fast rules for advertising practice. Before turning to the specific details of the study, in chapter 3, a brief overview of the findings and limitations of the complete study is presented as a means of orienting readers so they will not become lost in the details.

Overview of the Study and Findings

The purpose of the study was to address fundamental questions about advertising execution and measures of television advertising performance. To address these fundamental questions, two questions had to be addressed: (1) What is meant by an *executional device,* and how many are there? (2) What does *effectiveness* of a television commercial mean?

The development of the executional coding procedure is described in detail in chapter 3. The process involved an initial analysis of the marketing and advertising literature, examination of prior research, and discussions with representatives of both advertisers and advertising agencies. A preliminary list of 193 unique executional items was generated in this process, as well as numerous variations of certain items.

The initial pool of variables was used to code a set of 100 television commercials. This initial item pool was modified and refined and the coding process repeated until a set of items with acceptable interrater reliability was obtained. This set of 155 items represented the following categories of executional items, formats, and devices:

Information content,

Brand/product identification,

Setting,

Visual and auditory devices,

Promises/appeals/propositions,

Tone/atmosphere,

Comparisons,

Music and dancing,

Structure and format,

Characters,

Timing and counting measures (for example, length or number of times the brand name is shown or mentioned).

The measures of advertising performance employed in the study, as well as the set of commercials that formed the basis for the study, were provided by Research Systems Corporation. This commercial copy-testing firm was selected after an evaluation of twenty copy-testing services. Each of the twenty copy-testing services was contacted and asked for information concerning testing methodologies, procedures, reliability and validity of measures, and general research hygiene. These data have been summarized elsewhere (Stewart, Furse, and Kozak 1983). Research Systems Corporation used a laboratory copy-testing procedure to obtain three measures of advertising effectiveness: related recall, key message comprehension, and persuasion. Data concerning the reliability and validity of these measures are given in chapter 4.

After obtaining the cooperation of Research Systems Corporation, a sampling procedure was designed to obtain a representative set of commercials tested by the firm during the period 1980 to 1983. Coders were trained, given practice time, and provided a detailed coding guide (appendix A). Four independent coders evaluated each commercial selected by the sampling procedure. The dataset created by this procedure consisted of 1,059 commercials for 356 brands, 115 product categories, and 63 firms. Each commercial was coded on each of the 153 executional factors. Represented in the dataset were commercials for breakfast foods, beverages, entrees and side dishes, snack foods, household products, personal care products, over-the-counter drugs, and soft/hard goods (small appliances, mops, brooms, lamps). Recall scores for these commercials ranged from 5 to 80 percent, comprehension scores ranged from 0 to 68 percent, and persuasion scores (a brand-switching measure) ranged from −7 to 54 percent.

Before attempting to examine the relationship of particular executional variables and each of the performance measures, some basic data preparation was required. Executional variables were eliminated if they did not attain an average interrater reliability of .60 and occurred in less than 5 percent of the commercials. Product category effects were removed through the computation of residuals and the use of the Fair Share measure of Advertising Research System (ARS). Fair Share is an expected persuasion score based on product category and brand characteristics.

A series of regression analyses were run in an effort to understand the relationships between executional variables and each of the measures of advertising effectiveness. Executional variables appear to account for between 13 and 26 percent of the variance in related recall, depending on the specific analysis. Executional factors accounted for only about 8 percent of the variance in key message comprehension and 9 to 11 percent of the variance in persuasion. No single executional factor accounted for more than 6 percent of the variance of any measure. Both bivariate and multivariate relationships were examined in the study. The influence of factors such as whether the product was new or established and the level of switching in the category were also examined. These results suggest that care should be exercised when interpreting simple item-by-item relationships. The face validity, or most obvious interpretation, of a finding is not necessarily the most useful or defensible. In addition, the relationships are small and general, and clear exceptions to the pattern are easy to find. Nevertheless, the results obtained would appear to be consistent with much of the conventional wisdom of the advertising industry and theories of information processing.

Human beings cannot process more than a limited amount of information in a short time, particularly if the information is not understood or the viewer has little interest in it. Thus, the more information presented in the shorter time, the lower the expected recall. The following executional variables in the study were negatively related to recall because they relate to information load:

Information on components/ingredients,

Information on nutrition/health,

Research information,

Graphic displays,

Substantive supers,

Attributes/ingredients as main message,

Direct comparison with competitors,

Time (seconds) until product category identification,

Time (seconds) until brand name identification,

Time (seconds) until product/package is shown,

Total information,

Total propositions.

Executional variables in the study positively related to recall are associated with obtaining attention (novelty or humor), repetition, length of exposure, memory (memory aids), and vividness of information:

Brand-differentiating message,

Information on convenience of use,

Visual brand sign-off,

Setting directly related to product use,

Memorable rhyme/mnemonic device,

Cute/adorable tone,

Humorous tone,

Puffery (unsubstantiated comparison),

Demonstration (product use) format,

Demonstration (results) format,

Fantasy/surreal format,

Length of commercial,

Number of times brand name is mentioned,

Total time (seconds) product is on screen,

Number of times brand name/logo is on screen.

The single most important factor related to persuasion was the presence of an explicit brand-differentiating claim in the message. This is as much a result of basic product strategy as it is advertising execution, but this difference claim must be emphasized in the commercial to be effective.

Individual items negatively related to persuasion were:

Information on components/ingredients,

Information on nutrition/health,

Male principal character,

Background cast,

Outdoor setting,

Number of on-screen characters,

Total propositions,

Total psychological appeals (for example, comfort and safety).

Individual items positively related to persuasion were:

Brand-differentiating message,

Information on convenience of use,

Information on new product/new features,

Family-branded products,

Indirect comparison to competitors,

Demonstration (product use) format,

Demonstration (results) format,

Actor playing role as principal character,

No principal character,

Total time (seconds) product is on screen.

The results of the study support creative advertising philosophies that emphasize the uniqueness of the product. Brand-differentiating message was, by far, the single most important executional factor for explaining both recall and persuasion of a product. The presence of a brand-differentiating message was also found to be independent of the presence of other types of executional devices.

There were, however, some very important differences in the relationships among executional factors and measures of advertising effectiveness that were dependent on characteristics of the product being advertised. Brand-differentiating message was the single most important factor among commercials for established products but was not the most important factor among new product commercials. The presence of a brand-differentiating claim accounted for twice the variance in the persuasion measures among established product commercials than was accounted for among new product commercials. This finding is quite likely the result of the moderating influence of recall (and general product awareness). Results of the study found also that the presence of a brand-differentiating claim accounted for twice as much of the variation in persuasion when recall was high than when recall was low. The same executional variables influenced recall and persuasion performance of new product commercials, but for established products, the variables influencing recall and persuasion were largely independent of one another.

These differences between new and established product commercials suggest that the communication and persuasion process may not be the same for new product commercials as for established product commercials. Recall of a specific commercial appears to be much closer to the process of persuading viewers of new product commercials than recall is to persuading viewers of established products. For established products recall is much more likely to occur without persuasion and vice versa. The degree of brand switching in the product category appeared to have a similar moderating influence. Brand-differentiating message accounted for more variance in all three measures among commercials for products with higher category switching rates.

Prechoice, a surrogate measure for market share, also moderated the influence between executional factors and measures of advertising performance. Again, the largest impact was on the relationship between the presence of a brand-differentiating message and the measures of advertising performance. Brand-differentiating message accounted for substantially more variance in related recall and persuasion among commercials for established products with higher prechoice than among those with lower prechoice levels. Since higher prechoice brands are already better known to consumers before exposure, the results may suggest that prior brand awareness contributes to recall and persuasion of a specific advertising execution when an explicit differentiating claim is made, but prior awareness is considerably less likely to be an advantage if no brand-differentiating claim is made.

Details of the findings summarized in this chapter are provided in subsequent chapters. Relevant literature is cited in the discussion of these findings in an effort to show where the present results are consistent with other empirical studies and theoretical propositions.

Limitations of the Study

Empirical studies, whether carried out in the field or in the laboratory, and whether descriptive or a test of theory, suffer limitations that qualify the conclusions that may be drawn. In the present study the data represent a set of commercials tested by one copy-testing service during one particular time interval. For the most part, these commercials are for relatively inexpensive consumer packaged goods, although some small appliances and durables are also represented. The commercials tend to involve the use of balanced or positive appeals; few commercials in the dataset employ negative appeals. Appeals used in the commercials tend to be largely rational or a combination of rational and emotional appeals rather than primarily emotional. This is likely due to the nature of the products advertised in the commercials.

Another limitation of the dataset, and the conclusions that may be based on it, is related to the preselected nature of the commercials. The commercials in the dataset have reached a stage in development where the advertiser feels comfortable enough with the strategy and execution to carry out a test. Clearly inappropriate executional devices for a particular category or brand have been eliminated. This is one reason the present study failed to find significant crossover interactions. Executional factors that are clearly inappropriate for a particular product are unlikely to be present in the dataset.

The executional variables examined in the study are restricted to those that could be reliably coded. Other variables may be important, and these variables may, with further research, lend themselves to reliable coding. The set of executional factors used in this study is not exhaustive and may not include potentially important variables not identified in the code development stage of the research. Even among those variables that were examined in the present study, many appear so infrequently that useful analysis was not possible. It is likely that the frequency of executional devices changes over time. Some devices may become more important and frequent over time, while others may become less frequent or less important. Indeed, to the extent that future commercials become more homogeneous with respect to certain executional characteristics, those characteristics are less likely to differentiate commercials, and other executional variables, which manifest greater variability among commercials, will appear more important for differentiating commercials.

The data on which the current findings are based are aggregate data. The three measures of advertising performance are the sum of the reactions of several hundred viewers. Thus, the results may suggest much about the influence of executional factors at the macro level but do not provide an insight into the processes that occur at the level of the individual respondent. It is possible, and even likely, that a variety of different individual-level processes produce the types of aggregate results reported in the study. However, the results obtained are consistent with the results of other studies that have examined individual responses. Many of the same factors influencing recall, in both the positive and negative directions, have appeared in previous studies.

The present study emphasized characteristics of the advertising stimulus that may influence related recall, comprehension, or persuasion. It did not examine intervening constructs such as believability, relevance, production of counterarguments or other cognitive responses, or any of a variety of other viewer responses. These are measures of a response to a commercial rather than the characteristics of the commercial. As such, they represent further additional measures of advertising effectiveness that might be examined. These measures were not examined in the present study largely because they are intervening constructs. Characteristics of both the advertising stimulus and the individual interact to produce these measures. Examination of such measures would have required individual-level data that were not available and would have been extremely expensive to collect for sample sizes of the magnitude of those used in the present study.

The three measures of advertising effectiveness used in the study—related recall, key message comprehension, and persuasion—are specific measures developed by one commercial copy-testing service. While the demonstration of the reliability and validity of these measures appears to be as good as any in the industry, the validity of the persuasion measure for established products is based on a rather small number of observations. Other firms offer other measures, some with similar names, some that purport to measure the same factors as those measured by the three measures used in the present study. However, these other measures are often made operational in a different manner. Whether the results will generalize to these other measures is not clear. To the extent that other measures are reliable and valid for the same purpose, generalization should be appropriate.

A further limitation of the study is the nature of the respondent base from which the aggregate data were obtained. Advertisers specify the nature of the test audience. Most often the repondents from whom the data were obtained were current or potential product category users. While this is a strength of the data in many respects, it also restricts the generalization of the findings to consumers who have a predisposition toward using a product. The data say little about naive consumers or consumers not predisposed to purchase or use the product being advertised. The most frequent composition of the test audiences from whom the present data were drawn was all female, since women are the most frequent purchasers and users of the products advertised. A substantial number of the test audiences were of mixed sex, and a few were all male. There do not appear to be systematic effects related to audience composition in the study results.

The study examined the effect of a single exposure to a commercial. It did not examine the effects of multiple exposures to the same execution or several related executions. Long-term effects of advertising cannot be inferred from the results.

A final limitation of the study revolves around the question of causality. The study was designed as a descriptive study. As such, inferences of causality should be made with caution because the most obvious or simple interpretation of an executional factor may not be the best one. The effect of a particular executional factor may be the result of other unidentified factors that were not examined in the study. For example, the use of attribute/ingredient information in a commercial was found to be associated with both lower recall and persuasion scores. However, it is likely that this results because consumers often do not understand or want to use much of the attribute/ingredient information they are provided, not because the presentation of attribute/ingredient information in a commercial is inherently bad.

3
Executional Variables and Code Development

The first step in a study of advertising execution is the identification of appropriate executional factors and devices. This step is critical since it is important to define clearly each executional factor to be examined and to demonstrate that it can be reliably coded. To assure that future replications of findings are possible and to communicate more fully the nature of the findings to advertising researchers and professionals, operational definitions for each executional factor must be developed. The method by which executional factors used in the present study were identified, operationally defined, and examined for reliability is described in this chapter.

Method

Candidate Executional Variables

An initial list of advertising executional variables was generated from a literature review and informal discussions with advertising professionals. This initial list was submitted to a board of advertising professionals from several large national advertisers and advertising agencies. The board suggested other items and refinements of items already identified. Additional items were added over the course of the study as information was obtained from coding personnel. The total number of unique, individual executional variables examined during the code development process was 193. A number of items evolved over time, some items were combined, others were split into two or more parts.

Commercial Set

The commercials employed in the code development phase of the research were selected from various advertising agency reels. One hundred commercials were selected that were broadly representative of product categories, manufacturers, advertising agencies, and types of commercials. The majority of commercials were 30 seconds in length. About 10 percent were 60 seconds in length, one was 45 seconds, and two were 90 seconds in length. With the exception of several storyboards on film, all commercials were finished.

Coding Personnel

Fourteen individuals were employed during the various stages of code development. The majority of these was MBA students. Three were homemakers in the local community. The coding personnel ranged in age from the mid-twenties to early fifties. Both men and women served as coders.

Procedure

An initial informal phase of the research involved coders in a training and calibration task. Coders were asked to view commercials and complete an initial version of a coding guide. During this phase of the work, coders evaluated from ten to fifty commercials and were involved in a debriefing procedure that sought to identify problems with instructions, definitions, order of items, and items that should be added to the coding guide. No formal attempt was made to assess the reliability of the coding system during this phase of the work; rather, this work was primarily concerned with pretesting the coding guide and refining both the instructions and the items.

The second stage of code development involved a reliability check of individual items. Four coders evaluated one hundred commercials on 163 items. Reliability coefficients (coefficients of agreement, matching coefficients, or correlation coefficients) were computed for each pair of coders for each item. Coders were debriefed following the completion of their work and the computation of reliability coefficients. Each item was discussed with each coder, but particular emphasis was placed on items that did not appear to be reliable. Efforts were made to identify sources of unreliability in evaluations. Items involving counting and timing fared well in this stage, and because such items consumed about half the total time required to code a commercial, they were set aside for use in the final version of the coding guide.

Based on the results of the first round of reliability checks, items were modified, instructions changed, items rescaled, and other changes made in an effort to improve items. A second coding form, consisting of 130 items, was generated. Five coders (including the three homemakers) who had not previously been exposed to the commercials viewed and coded fifty commercials. Interrater reliabilities were computed for each pair of coders, and the coders were debriefed in an effort to identify sources of unreliability.

Twenty-eight items failed to obtain sufficient reliability in either round of coding. Items that were confused with one another but that were otherwise reliable in the first reliability check were combined into a single item. For example, "economy" and "savings" and "customer satisfaction" and "customer dedication/loyalty" were commonly confused in the first round of coding and were combined in the second round. A high degree of reliability was obtained for these composite items in the second round of coding.

The final version of the coding guide, which includes only items obtaining acceptable reliability in this phase of the research, is given in appendix A. Detailed definitions of each item are provided in the coding guide. The final version of the coding guide includes twenty-six different types of information; types of appeals; timing and counting variables such as commercial length, time until the product is identified, and number of characters; structure and format of the commercial; music; visual and auditory memory devices; commercial atmosphere and tone; commercial setting; and presence of a brand-differentiating claim.

Appendix B lists the items that did not achieve sufficient reliability for inclusion in the final coding system. In general, the items that failed to achieve sufficient reliability fell into five major categories: (1) items related to production quality, (2) items related to believability, (3) items calling for some type of evaluative judgment about the commercial, (4) items related to the congruence of commercial elements, and (5) a miscellaneous set of items. A brief discussion of these items and the problems associated with them follows.

Quality. Several of the coders had either agency experience or training in drama or radio and television production. Even these individuals were not able to arrive at reliable evaluations of commercial quality. Debriefing provided the reasons. The set of commercials used in the project tended to be very homogeneous with respect to quality; almost all had appeared on the air. Thus, efforts at scaling production quality tended to produce artifactual results based more on personal preference for production techniques than quality. In addition, there was some disagreement concerning what constituted quality. For example, for one commercial a coder suggested that the technical qualities of video and voice were poor compared to other commercials. Another coder suggested the same commercial represented high quality of production (in a holistic sense) since the video and audio reinforced the message of the commercial. The great majority of commercials simply could not be differentiated reliably on the basis of quality. Most commercials are reasonably homogeneous on this dimension, given that advertising agencies do a signficant amount of self-censorship prior to the client's initiating copy testing and the fact that quality within the form of a commercial was the focus of these items.

Quality is a function of not only the production characteristics of the commercial but also the medium on which the commercial is viewed. Older VCRs (video cassette recorders) and monitors tended to produce poorer quality pictures and sound than a new, commercial quality VCR and monitor. Ultimately, only the latter equipment was used for coding the quality items. One implication of this finding is that the quality of a commercial viewed by an individual household will be a function of the type and age of television set.

Believability and Evaluation. These items seem to represent measures of commercial performance rather than characteristics of the commercials. The sources of unreliability in these items were related to characteristics of the coding personnel such as age, sex, and prior product use. Thus, the characteristics of the commercials appeared to be interacting with the characteristics of the viewers to produce responses to these items. It was to detect just this source of variability that the varied set of coders used in the project was selected.

Congruence of Commercial Elements. There appears to be a strong element of evaluation in these items. Items related to characters fitting the product or commercial storyline seemed to tap the degree of empathy the coders experienced and their knowledge of and experience with the product category and, in some cases, the character(s) in the commercial. The issues of executional versus message content dominance and congruence of audio and video were dependent on what the coders thought the primary message of the commercial was intended to be. Thus, one coder would argue for congruence under the assumption of one intent while another would argue that congruence did not exist under a different assumption. Coders also found it difficult to separate the audio and video messages.

A reliable coding of these items would probably require an extremely time-consuming procedure involving three sets of raters. One set of raters would only hear the commercial; another set would only view the commercial. Each set of raters would describe their interpretation of the message obtained. A third set of judges would then rate the degree of congruence between the two sets of ratings. While these are interesting items, the amount of effort required was beyond the scope and resources of the study.

Miscellaneous. These items appear to require a knowledge of the product category, inference, or both. Coders had difficulty separating the number of sales points (benefits) from supporting evidence and other information. The continuing claim variable appeared to be systematically related to prior product knowledge and experience. Judging whether the primary sales point was stated or inferred was a problem for many coders. Coders indicated that they almost always inferred something more about the sales point from the commercial than was explicitly stated.

Developing and Coding the Database

Relatively few firms have available a dataset containing commercials in sufficiently large numbers and with sufficient diversity of products to provide an opportunity for assessing the effects of advertising execution. Further complicating the task of identifying a suitable data source was the need for comparable measures for all commercials and demonstrated reliability and validity of the measures of advertising effectiveness. These needs eliminated the option of obtaining data from a single manufacturer or advertising agency. Most previous research has been carried out by advertising copy-testing services so a suitable data source was sought from this group of firms.

Each of twenty advertising copy-testing firms was contacted and asked for information concerning their copy-testing service. Information was sought on sampling procedures, testing methodology, reliability and validity of measures, and other relevant details of their service. The details of these contacts and a description of the information obtained are provided by Stewart, Furse, and Kozak (1983). Based on both the information obtained and the thoroughness of documentation, Research Systems Corporation was identified as a candidate source of data. Research Systems Corporation agreed to cooperate in the study by providing access to their bank of previously tested commercial tapes and by supplying three measures of advertising effectiveness for each commercial. Chapter 4 provides details on Research Systems Corporation, their methodology for copy testing, and their measures of advertising effectiveness.

Selection of Commercials for Coding and Analysis

A random sample of commercials tested by Research Systems Corporation was selected for coding. Commercials in the sampling frame were those tested between 1980 and 1983, inclusive, and for which all three measures of advertising effectiveness were available. Commercials were excluded from the sampling frame if they were not submitted to Research Systems Corporation's standard testing procedure. A total of 1,059 commercials were ultimately selected for use in the study.

Description of Commercials

The commercials present in the dataset represented 63 companies, 115 product categories, and 356 individual brands. Forty-seven percent of the commercials were for new or improved products or line extensions. Fifty-three percent were for established products. No single manufacturer accounted for more than 14 percent of the commercials. Firms represented in more than 5 percent of the commercials tended to be large diversified companies offering products in a wide range of categories. No single product accounted for more than twenty (2 percent) of the commercials in the dataset. No single product category accounted for more than 6 percent of the commercials.

To assess product effects, as well as to describe more fully the commercials in the dataset, twelve global product categories were identified. Each commercial was categorized as being for a product in one of the following classes:

Breakfast foods (cereals, breakfast bars);

Beverages (milk, wine, soft drinks);

Entrees and side dishes (frozen entrees, vegetables);

Snack foods and desserts (cakes, chips, dips, candies);

Other food products (not one of the preceding);

Over-the-counter remedies (pain relievers, cough syrups);

Other over-the-counter products (vitamins, supplements);

Cleaners/solvents/sprays/shiners;

Other household products (paper goods);

Personal hygiene products (shampoo, toothpaste, deodorant);

Other personal care products (cosmetics);

Soft/hard goods (small appliances, durables).

These categories provided relatively homogeneous groups of products made up of sufficiently large numbers of commercials to permit within-category analyses. Table 3–1 provides a detailed description of the composition of the twelve categories. Each of these categories contained commercials for direct competitors and companies offering multiple products in one or more subcategories. The diversity of brands, products, categories, and firms within each of the global categories helped assure that results were not driven by advertising strategies employed by a single firm or for a specific brand.

Coding

The coding guide contained 141 dichotomous or trichotomous items and fourteen additional items involving timing, counting, product category, and degree of finish. All 1,059 commercials were coded on each of these 155 items. The personnel employed for coding were experienced coders. Each coder received training and approximately 20 hours of practice time prior to beginning the coding process. Four coders evaluated each dichotomous and trichotomous item. Two raters completed the remaining fourteen timing and

Table 3–1
Product Groups in Dataset

Product Category	Number in Group	Description	Percent of Commercials for New or Improved Products	Percent of Live Commercials
I. Breakfast foods	52	26 different products offered by 7 different companies	35	80
II. Beverages	46	18 different products offered by 7 different companies	17	69
III. Entrees and side dishes	68	35 different products offered by 16 different companies	27	84
IV. Snack foods	39	22 different products offered by 3 different companies	44	60
V. Other foods	186	62 different products offered by 12 different companies	40	54
VI. Over-the-counter remedies	145	50 different products offered by 10 different companies	50	90
VII. Other over-the-counter products	100	40 different products offered by 16 different companies	58	70
VIII. Cleaners/solvents/sprays/shiners	122	40 different products offered by 8 different companies	35	70
IX. Other household products	75	46 different products offered by 9 different companies	55	61
X. Personal hygiene products	38	18 different products offered by 8 different companies	82	85
XI. Other personal care products	63	43 different products offered by 18 different companies	61	69
XII. Soft/hard goods	61	29 different products offered by 14 different companies	18	90

counting items. Each coder required approximately ½ hour to complete the coding of a commercial, which usually involved viewing the commercial several times. Slightly more than 2,000 labor-hours were required to complete the coding phase of the study.

Coders were instructed to evaluate commercials based solely on the advertising stimuli present; that is, they were instructed not to make inferences. For example, they were instructed to code commercials as having a unique claim (brand-differentiating message) if it was clear from the commercial that the claim was unique. The only exception to these instructions was made for continuing executional elements (continuing character or music) where some prior knowledge was required for coding.

Reliabilities and Frequencies of Executional Items

Interrater reliabilities were computed for all items in the dataset. Appendix C provides the average interrater reliability coefficients for both dichotomous (gamma coefficients) and trichotomous (contingency coefficients) items. Pearson product moment correlation coefficients are reported for all timing and counting items.

Composite codes for each item on each commercial were created by taking the average of the two raters for all timing and counting items. For dichotomous and trichotomous items, the majority opinion of the four raters was used to assign a value to each executional code. For those items where a 50-50 split occurred among raters, a missing value code was assigned. Appendix C reports the frequencies with which each executional code occurred in the overall dataset.

Approximately one-third of the items failed to appear in more than 2 percent of the commercials (twenty commercials), and only about half of the executional items occurred in more than 5 percent of the commercials. There was a tendency for low reliability items to be concentrated among items that occurred infrequently, which is a common occurrence in reliability studies. It is likely that if some items occurred more frequently, their reliabilities would have been higher. Results obtained from unreliable and/or infrequently occurring items should not be regarded as substantive. With the few exceptions noted later, only items obtaining a reliability of .60 and a frequency of occurrence of at least 5 percent (fifty commercials) were used in further analyses. An important reason for adopting this rule was related to executional variable/product category confounding. A number of infrequently observed items were totally or partially confounded with one of the twelve product category groupings. Two items, "infants and children as main characters" and "animals as main characters," occurred in more than 5 percent of the commercials but were still completely confounded with product category.

Appendix D provides a breakdown of each of the executional codes by product category. Several attempts were made to identify subsets of commercials exhibiting similar patterns of executional factors. These attempts were not successful, but are briefly described in the following.

Clustering Commercials by Executional Similarity

Commercials for the same product, tested at roughly the same time, tend to look very much alike. Hierarchical cluster analysis (Ward's procedure) of principal components derived from executional items tended to produce large numbers of two- and three-member clusters, composed of commercials for the same brand, tested at approximately the same time. This is perhaps not surprising since it might be expected that commercials for the same product will resemble one another, particularly if each execution grows from an overall product communication strategy. This does seem to suggest that firms using Research Systems Corporation's testing method tend to be testing variants of the same strategy or theme rather than fundamentally different brand strategies.

There was also a tendency for some competitive products in the same subcategory to resemble one another. A definitive test of similarity was not possible because the numbers of competitive products in the database were not sufficiently large to provide a verifiable and stable clustering solution. An interesting point that emerged is that competitive brands offered by the same firms tended to be less similar than competitive products offered by different firms. This may suggest that firms (at least those with multiple products) are better able to differentiate their own products from one another than from competitive products. It is not surprising that similar products appear to have similar commercials since it is likely that benefits and executional devices appropriate for one such product may also be appropriate for a competing product.

While these results are interesting and raise some important questions, definitive answers must await a larger database that includes very large numbers of competitive products. It would also have been interesting to examine subsets of commercials that were similar along the full range of executional variables examined in the study. Unfortunately, the clustering algorithms employed in the study failed to identify large subsets of such commercials, and where such subsets were identified, they tended to be identifiable as particular brands or products.

4
Dependent Measures of Advertising Effectiveness: Related Recall, Comprehension, and Persuasion

Research Systems Corporation Methodology

Commercial Exposure and Sample

Research Systems Corporation employs an off-air method for testing commercials, called the *advertising research system* (ARS). Each test commercial is exposed in regular test sessions to men and women whose names are randomly drawn from telephone directories covering the Detroit, Baltimore, San Francisco, and Houston metropolitan areas and who are invited by mail to preview two typical half hours of television material. (See appendix E for a discussion of the sampling procedures employed by RSC.) Each test commercial is edited into program material with eleven other unrelated commercials. Approximately 525 individuals view each test commercial, which usually results in a usable sample of 300 to 450 respondents. Client organizations specify the character of respondents tabulated for their test. Most often targeted respondents are characteristic of current or potential users of the product category for which the specific commercial is representative.

Measures of Advertising Effectiveness

Persuasion. Persuasion refers to the ability of the commercial to persuade consumers to prefer the advertised brand. This measure is obtained by asking respondents to indicate brand preference before and after exposure to programs and commercials (a period of approximately 2 hours elapses between these tests). On both measurement occasions respondents are asked to indicate which brand they would like if they were the winner of a drawing. Products are presented in photographs that resemble store shelf placements. Both the product that is presented in the test commercial and competitive products (including private store brands) are presented in the photograph.

The persuasion measure is the percentage of respondents choosing the test brand over the competition after exposure to the television material minus the percentage choosing the test brand before exposure. This is a *raw persuasion* measure. This measure may be contrasted with the *expected* pre-post switching for the brand given no exposure to the test commercial. This *expected* level of persuasion is called *Fair Share* (a service mark of Research Systems Corporation) and is discussed later.

Related Recall. Three days after exposure to the television material and test commercials, respondents are contacted by telephone. Respondents are given the opportunity to claim recall on the basis of a product category cue, then a brand cue. Recall questioning is carried out only for those who claim to have remembered the test commercial. The related recall measure is the percentage of respondents who claim to have seen, and can give playback related to, the test commercial.

Respondents have demonstrated related recall if:

They provide playback uniquely related to the test commercial only.

They provide playback uniquely related to the test commercial and any other playback.

They provide playback of only general recall, or when generally related is equal to or outweighs generally unrelated recall.

Key Message Comprehension. Key message comprehension is measured during the same interview in which related recall is obtained. It is a measure of a special type of recall—namely, recall of the specified key message of the test commercial. The key message is identified by Research Systems Corporation staff prior to commercial testing. Key message comprehension is the percentage of respondents who play back the identified primary message of the commercial.

Reliability of Related Recall and Persuasion Measures

Research Systems Corporation publishes summaries of the results of their in-house research hygiene program. This program (ARS automatic retest) selects every Nth commercial for retesting within a 3-week interval of the original client-sponsored test. Test-retest reliability may be examined through this procedure. Since Research Systems Corporation publishes actual values of the test and retest measures, it is possible to verify independently the reliability of the measures, assuming that the data provided are accepted at face value.

The ARS automatic retest data manifest a test-retest reliability coefficient of .91 for recall and .93 for persuasion. Two other reliability analyses may be used to determine if a significant amount of variance due to biases is present.

Table 4–1
Test-Retest Reliability of Persuasion and Recall

	Persuasion		Recall	
	Observed Variation	Expected Variation	Observed Variation	Expected Variation
σ	1.75	1.74	3.48	3.18
σ^2	3.06	3.03	12.11	10.11
F ratio	1.02		1.19	
Number of pairs	58		67	
F values necessary for significance at the 95% significance level	1.33		1.31	

The first is an *F* test, using the ratio of observed variance (total test-retest variance) to expected sampling variance. Ratios close to 1 suggest that there is little or no extraneous variance in the system; ratios that are significantly larger than 1 indicate the presence of non-random-sampling error or uncontrolled biases. Tabled values for the *F* distribution may be used to determine how much larger than 1 an *F* ratio must be for significance at the 95 percent level of significance.

The results of a recent ARS analysis are presented in table 4–1. Neither *F* ratio is significant, indicating that:

1. The ARS system is about as reliable as the laws of random sampling allow.

2. It contains little extraneous bias variance causing one test result to differ from another. This does not mean that test-retest results will never differ. Some differences will always occur by chance alone. These differences should be rare, however.

The second analysis examines the distribution of differences between the individual pairs of test-retest commercials. If the measure is reliable, the distribution of differences should be approximately the same as that expected by chance. In this case, the differences are expressed as *t* values:

$$t \text{ value} = \frac{(\text{test score}) - (\text{retest score})}{\text{standard error of difference}}.$$

When sampling error alone is operating, the distribution of test-retest *t* values will match the distribution as found in a standard table of *t* values. For example, if there were one hundred test-retest comparisons, then random sampling error alone would call for ten significant differences at the 10 percent level of significance. If many more than ten are found, then the system has more variation than would be expected from random sampling alone, and the results will indicate the presence of biases. The statistical procedure that can indicate the presence of significant biases compares the actual test-retest distribution of *t* values to the known sampling distribution using a chi-square goodness of fit test. In industry practice, standard tests for significant differences between commercials are performed at the 10 percent level of significance, so the 10 percent cutoff is used in this analysis. The chi-square goodness of fit tests between the expected and actual distributions shown in the following are not significantly different, indicating the absence of variation due to systematic biases in the measurement system. This lack of significance also indicates that the distribution of paired differences between commercial tests follows the *t* distribution. Thus, it is appropriate to use standard *t* tests when evaluating persuasion or recall levels. (See table 4–2.)

Validity of Related Recall. Research Systems Corporation has published data indicating that their related recall measure is highly correlated with more traditional day-after on-air recall measures (Research Systems Corporation 1982). For some forty pairs of commercials, where both related recall and on-air day-after recall are available, related recall scores predicted on-air scores as well as the on-air scores predicted themselves (.83 and .82 respec-

Table 4–2
Analysis of the Distribution of Recall and Persuasion Scores

		Persuasion		Recall	
t Value	*Expected Percent of Cases*	*Expected Number of Cases*	*Actual Number of Cases*	*Expected Number of Cases*	*Actual Number of Cases*
0.000–0.674	50	29	31	33.5	31
0.675–0.842	10	5.8	2	6.7	8
0.843–1.036	10	5.8	4	6.7	8
1.037–1.282	10	5.8	7	6.7	3
1.283–1.644	10	5.8	10	6.7	7
1.645–1.959	5	2.9	2	3.35	5
>1.960	5	2.9	2	3.35	5
Observed X^2 for 10 percent cutoff		7.3		4.37	
X^2 needed for significance		11.07		11.07	
(df = 5, 10% level of significance)		Not significant		Not significant	

tively.) Also, in thirty-one test markets for new products, related recall was shown to be related to advertising-generated levels of awareness ($r = .78$) when levels of awareness are corrected for media weight. These latter data refer only to new brands entering existing markets and where the brand was a nondurable packaged good.

Validity of Persuasion. Research Systems Corporation has available a substantial amount of data indicating a strong relationship between their persuasion measure and trial rates for new products (Research Systems Corporation 1983a). The correlation between the persuasion measure and actual trial rate in thirty-one test markets for new products is .85. Further, the correlation between the persuasion measure and the trial rate predicted by a frequently employed new product model, Assessor (Silk and Urban 1978), is .90. The amount of validation data available for established brands is not as plentiful but is also supportive (Research Systems Corporation 1983b). In split-cable studies involving commercials with significant differences in persuasion measures, there was a corresponding difference in sales. Further, in those markets employing different media weights, commercials with low levels of persuasion led to no measurable increases in sales, regardless of media weight, while high persuasion levels led to significant increases in sales with increased media weight. Unfortunately, eleven of these cases employed low-persuasion commercials, and only three cases were high persuasion, so the data are limited.

Reliability and Validity of Comprehension Measure

The reliability of the ARS comprehension measure has not been established, but the measure is highly correlated with related recall (.70 +). Validity has also not been established primarily because it is not clear what the appropriate criterion measure would be.

In summary, strongly supportive data are available for the reliability of both the related recall and persuasion measures. The validity of these measures for awareness and trial of new products is also reasonably well established. Validity for established brands is suggested, but few data are available at this time. Generally, the reliability and validity data are as good or better than any measures currently available in the advertising copy-testing industry (see Stewart, Furse, and Kozak 1983, for a review of these issues).

Correcting Persuasion for Product-Specific Effects

There are without doubt product-specific differences within the related recall, comprehension, and persuasion measures. To assess the impact of

Table 4–3
Product Category Differences in Persuasion Scores

	Category A		Category B		Category C
Brand	Mean Persuasion	Brand	Mean Persuasion	Brand	Mean Persuasion
A	3%	AA	2%	A	−2%
B	12	B	4	B	7
C	12	C	18	C	13
Category norm = 9		Category norm = 8		Category norm = 6	

Table 4–4
Effects of Market Share on Persuasion Scores

	Category A			Category B			Category C	
Brand	Market Share	Mean Persuasion	Brand	Market Share	Mean Persuasion	Brand	Market Share	Mean Persuasion
A	45%	3%	A	44%	2%	A	45%	−2%
B	11	12	B	22	4	B	11	7
C	10	12	C	New	18	C	New	13

executional factors on these measures, it is first necessary to remove these product-specific effects. As noted earlier, unless these effects are removed, it is not possible to assess accurately the effects of advertising execution alone, since execution and product category will be confounded. A common method for dealing with category effects is comparison of the results for a particular commercial to some norm, or historical average, for the category. As noted in chapter 2, using such norms creates a number of problems. For example, when the interest is to examine cross-category effects like in the present study, the computation of an index (or other transformation) relative to a category norm creates data that are no longer directly comparable. Also, category-based norms may produce unusual results. Consider the example in table 4–3. Note that each category has brands that score at, above, and below that category norm. It may be reasonable to assume that some brands consistently score below the norm while others consistently score above the norm. This would result from nonadvertising influences on the sales effectiveness or persuasion measure. For example, consider the influence of market share as shown in table 4–4. It is clear that market share is probably related to the persuasion scores. In this example, high market share results in lower persuasion scores. If more prospects pick the high-share brand at the beginning of the test, there are fewer customers who can switch to the high share product at the end of the test and more who can switch from the product. The reverse situation occurs for new products since there can only be a switch to the new product.

Research Systems Corporation's measure, Fair Share, is designed to correct for these effects. Fair Share is designed to provide, for each brand, an equitable basis for comparison. It represents the level of switching to and from a brand that would be expected for the particular competitive environment even without advertising exposure. The Fair Share score is applied to the persuasion measure to adjust for both category and brand-specific factors.

Fair Share

Fair Share is used to understand the effects of three factors on the persuasion measure (Research Systems Corporation 1984):

Brand-switching proportion, which is used to estimate the number of nonloyals in the particular category;

The number of brands competing in the market for those nonloyals;

The size of the test brand's share of the market or franchise strength of the brand.

Brand-Switching Proportion. A certain proportion of respondents change their brand choices from the pre-exposure measure to the postexposure measure, much like they do from one purchase occasion to the next. This proportion of respondents is called a *switching proportion*. There is a great range in the switching proportions across product categories, while the switching proportion is relatively stable within a product category. It has been demonstrated through numerous tests that the larger the product class switching proportion, the larger the resulting ARS persuasion scores; that is, the more switchers, or nonloyals, that are available to be persuaded, the greater potential there is for persuasion.

Number of Brands in the Market. In addition to the brand-switching proportion, persuasion scores are influenced by the number of brands competing in the product class. In general, the more brands from which the switchers, or nonloyals, may select, the smaller the number of switchers who will select any one brand, so persuasion scores are depressed.

Franchise Strength. In general, the proportion of the sample that chooses a brand prior to exposure to the test commercial is fairly representative of the brand's share of the product class market. This is referred to as a brand's franchise strength. The bigger the brand's share of the market (for example, the higher the prechoice measure), the lower the expected persuasion scores (postchoice minus prechoice percentage). A brand with a large market share has a smaller pool of available switchers in the test from which to draw and a larger pool of switchers who may select another brand in the postchoice situation.

Information on switching rates, number of brands competing in the market, and franchise strength may be used to calculate an expected persuasion score. It has been shown that this computed rate of expected switching is highly associated with observed switching rates in the absence of advertising exposure. The persuasion scores observed in testing may be compared to the specific brand's Fair Share, and an interpretation of the effect of the commercial is based on the difference between the actual outcome and the expected outcome. Commercials that significantly outscore their Fair Share are superior commercials in that they did better than expected. Likewise, commercials that score significantly below their Fair Share can be said to have done less well than expected. This provides a basis for comparing persuasion measures across categories since each measure can be corrected not only for category effects but also brand-specific effects. In summary, the Fair Share concept is useful because it eliminates the misuse of norms, particularly category norms. Some brands typically exceed the category norm while others fall far below. Given their respective franchise strengths, however, they might all be performing at or above their Fair Share.

Product Category Effects and Recall and Comprehension

Unfortunately, no measure comparable to Fair Share has been developed for related recall or key message comprehension. Thus, no expected value is available for these two measures. For that reason, other methods were used to correct for category effects.

Characteristics of the Database with Respect to Measures of Advertising Effectiveness

Table 4–5 provides a descriptive breakdown of the recall, comprehension, and persuasion measures for the total dataset and each of the twelve product categories. Table 4–6 provides a descriptive breakdown of prechoice, switching, and number of brands in each category and in the overall dataset. Substantial category differences exist for recall, comprehension, and raw persuasion. Over-the-counter product commercials tend to be quite low, relative to the overall dataset, on all three measures. Commercials in the soft-hard

Table 4–5
Advertising Effectiveness Measures, by Product Category

	Recall		Comprehension		Raw Persuasion	
	Mean	Standard Deviation	Mean	Standard Deviation	Mean	Standard Deviation
Breakfast foods	30.61	11.39	15.25	10.79	4.56	3.36
Beverages	28.85	9.43	10.10	7.33	4.77	3.44
Entrees and side dishes	30.30	12.77	12.58	11.21	8.79	10.59
Snack foods	34.73	13.36	18.35	15.49	12.10	10.07
Other food products	32.81	13.49	12.76	9.33	5.53	5.97
Over-the-counter remedies	22.75	7.46	9.68	6.54	3.90	3.98
Other over-the-counter products	22.96	11.67	10.60	7.66	5.13	4.59
Cleaners/solvents/sprays/shiners	32.17	11.67	17.02	12.30	9.05	7.13
Other household products	36.96	14.51	22.35	16.24	14.02	12.55
Personal hygiene products	28.62	11.39	14.34	10.57	6.24	4.34
Other personal care products	24.18	9.83	9.62	7.69	5.31	3.54
Soft/hard goods	38.13	15.17	22.36	15.99	7.75	7.26
All products	29.76	11.91	13.97	11.52	6.80	7.30

Table 4–6
Product and Brand Characteristics, by Product Category

	Prechoice		Switching Proportion		Number of Competitors in Test		N
	Mean	Standard Deviation	Mean	Standard Deviation	Mean	Standard Deviation	
Breakfast foods	8.10	11.13	30.09	5.48	15.06	7.15	57
Beverages	12.40	9.74	28.98	5.23	9.13	3.54	48
Entrees and side dishes	19.23	19.74	25.45	10.47	6.94	2.62	69
Snack foods	6.98	11.76	37.54	7.14	9.26	4.56	40
Other food products	10.71	14.75	25.25	5.78	9.95	4.33	197
Over-the-counter remedies	8.31	9.87	24.56	4.95	10.22	2.68	155
Other over-the-counter products	6.90	12.01	25.24	4.48	11.26	3.43	106
Cleaners/solvents/sprays/shiners	16.47	23.17	28.57	7.45	6.93	2.58	124
Other household products	8.74	13.52	32.53	9.03	7.26	2.97	78
Personal hygiene products	4.97	10.87	22.72	4.21	9.04	3.73	47
Other personal care products	4.98	9.92	25.12	3.76	11.44	4.00	73
Soft/hard goods	16.95	15.68	27.95	6.15	11.56	5.86	64
All products	10.62	14.64	27.02	6.34	9.72	4.40	1,059

goods category and other household product categories tend to be higher than other categories on both recall and comprehension. It is clear that product category differences exist, and these differences cannot be attributed to the greater frequency of new products in some categories. Differences persist even when new/improved products are eliminated from the analysis.

The use of the Fair Share measure to adjust the persuasion score appears to remove much of the category and brand-specific effects from this measure, although some differences still exist. These differences may be largely attributed to the simple subtraction procedure used to obtain the adjusted persuasion measure. Subtraction does not fully remove confounding sources of variation. Only some form of covariance analysis (a decidedly more complex procedure) will accomplish this end. Further, Fair Share is a brand-specific measure of expected switching. Thus, it will not necessarily fully eliminate category differences where these exist.

Elimination of Product Category Effects from Measures of Advertising Effectiveness

To examine the influence of category effects on each of the three measures of advertising effectiveness, a series of regression analyses were performed. Dummy variables, each representing one of the twelve product categories, were created. These dummy variables were then used as independent variables to predict related recall, comprehension, and persuasion.

Sixteen percent of the variance in related recall was accounted for by the product category variables. Thirteen percent of the variance in comprehension and 15 percent of the variance in raw (unadjusted) persuasion were accounted for by the product dummy variables. The effectiveness of the Fair Share measure was supported by the finding that only 8 percent of the variance in the adjusted persuasion measure was accounted for by product category.

To remove the effects of product category from further analyses, residual scores were computed for each of the three measures, removing the variance attributable to membership in one of the twelve product categories. This procedure does not, however, remove variance attributable to specific subcategories of products or to specific brands. As noted earlier, the adjusted persuasion measure provides a vehicle for removing this additional variance from the persuasion score, but no comparable procedure is available for adjusting recall or comprehension.

The results reported are quite robust. Few differences from the findings using the original Research System Corporation scores arose when using the residual scores. Where such differences did arise, they were related to the raw persuasion measure, and the Fair Share adjusted persuasion measure appeared to be adequate for resolving most of these problems.

Relationships among Recall, Comprehension, and Persuasion Measures

The three measures of advertising performance were not independent of one another. Recall and comprehension were not surprisingly highly correlated (.71), and recall and comprehension were more modestly correlated with persuasion. Recall had a correlation of .31 with persuasion, while comprehension had a .33 correlation with persuasion. These correlation coefficients are based on residual scores (product category effects have been removed), but similar coefficients were obtained with the original measures (.73 for recall and comprehension, .33 for recall and persuasion, .40 for comprehension and persuasion). These relationships among measures do not necessarily hold for all types of products. New and improved product commercials and those for line extensions manifest a somewhat different relationship between recall and comprehension and persuasion from that found in the data for established/non-new-product commercials. The correlation coefficients for recall and comprehension are virtually identical for new and established products: .72 and .69 respectively. There is a much stronger relationship between both recall and persuasion and comprehension and persuasion for new products commercials. New product commercial recall and persuasion scores had a correlation coefficient of .42, while recall and persuasion for established product commercials had a correlation of only .22. Comprehension and persuasion among new product commercials had a .43 correlation, and in established product commercials they had a .28 correlation. Persuasion appeared to be more closely associated with recall and comprehension for new product commercials but to operate more independently for established product commercials.

Brand and Category Factors and Their Relationship to Measures of Advertising Effectiveness

The three brand and category factors used to estimate the Fair Share measure—brand-swithing proportion, number of brands, and franchise strength— were related to one or more of the advertising performance measures. Table 4–7 provides the correlations among these factors. The table illustrates that the switching proportion—that is, the number of nonloyal customers—is strongly related to the persuasion measure. The higher the switching proportion, the higher the obtained persuasion score. Brand fran-

Table 4–7
Relationships among Brand-Switching Proportion, Number of Brands, Franchise Strength, and Measures of Advertising Performance

	Recall	*Comprehension*	*Persuasion*
Brand-switching proportion	.06	.15	.63
Brand franchise (prechoice)	.19	.12	−.31
Number of brands	−.17	−.22	−.20

Note: All three advertising measures are residual scores obtained by removing the effects of product category membership.

chise, or market share, is negatively related to persuasion, and it also manifests a significant, but low, correlation with both recall and comprehension. Number of competing brands has a uniformly negative correlation with each of the measures of advertising performance. The larger the number of competing brands, the lower the recall, comprehension, and persuasion scores. All these relationships are consistent both with conventional wisdom in the marketing discipline and the computation of the Fair Share measure. Consumers are more likely to remember commercials for products they have used, so recall and comprehension are positively related to brand franchise. When there are large numbers of brands competing for the consumer's attention, consumers may be less likely to recall the advertising for a specific brand. Thus, number of brands is negatively related to both recall and comprehension.

The three brand-category factors also manifest relationships with each other that are consistent with conventional wisdom. Switching proportion is negatively related to brand franchise ($r = -.36$); the higher the prechoice for any given brand, the lower the category switching rate. Brand franchise is also negatively related to number of brands ($r = -.39$); the greater the number of brands available within a category, the lower the prechoice for any given brand. Switching proportion and number of brands appear to be relatively independent ($r = .04$). This would suggest that the amount of switching in a category is dependent on factors other than the mere availability of larger numbers of alternatives.

5
Bivariate Relationships

Description of Executional Characteristics of the Dataset

Most commercials contained information on product quality, components or ingredients, superiority, and results of using the product. Virtually all were for a single product, and the vast majority had visual and auditory brand sign-offs.

Appendix C describes the reliability and frequency of occurrence of all executional variables in the 1,059-commercial database. The bivariate relationships of each executional variable with recall, comprehension, and persuasion are also reported in appendix C.

Most commercials focused on product performance and/or attributes or ingredients and featured balanced emotional and rational appeals. Unsubstantiated, nonspecific claims of product superiority (puffery) were favored over either direct or indirect product comparisons. The majority favored product demonstration using either male or female principal on-screen characters with a voice-over. Most commercials were depicted in an indoor setting.

Information occurring in a significant minority of commercials in the database was sensory information (how the product tastes, feels, or smells), information on new products or new features, information on nutrition and health, user satisfaction, and convenience of use. A significant number of commercials were for family-branded products and for products whose brand name reinforced the product application. About one in five utilized no recognizable setting for the commercial.

Product reminder was the main message in about one of every four commercials. Those with primarily rational appeals outnumbered those with primarily emotional appeals by four to one, although two-thirds of the commercials were characterized by a balance of rational and emotional appeals. Just under half the commercials made a specific brand-differentiating claim— an explicit claim that only the advertised product had a particular ingredient, could perform a particular function, and so on.

The most popular commercial tones or atmosphere were modern/contemporary, conservative/traditional, and relaxed/comfortable. Indirect product comparisons occurred more than twice as frequently as direct comparisons with named competitors. Mood- or image-dominant commercials were almost one-third of the total, followed by demonstration-of-results and problem/solution formats.

More than a third of the over 150 executional variables tested occurred in less than 5 percent, or approximately 50, of the total 1,059 commercials. These variables have been excluded from further analysis and discussion, except when they have been used to construct composite variables.

The dominant commercial length in the dataset is 30 seconds, and the brand name is mentioned and shown visually an average of four times. On average, 5 to 7 seconds elapse after the start of the commercial before the product category and brand name are revealed. The product is on screen an average of 17 seconds, and the package, brand name, or logo is on for 14 seconds. The vast majority of commercials in the database delivered the principal message within the first 10 seconds.

Bivariate Relationships

Specific executional variables were selected for discussion and further analysis based on the following criteria: (1) average intercoder reliability coefficient of at least .60; (2) frequency of occurrence of at least 5 percent, or 50 commercials; and (3) 95 percent significance level for the measure of association between the executional variable and one or more of the performance measures. When an executional variable demonstrated a relationship with recall, comprehension, or persuasion at the 95 percent significance level, any other relationships down to the 90 percent significance level were also cited.

The statistics for the relationships between the executional variables and the dependent, performance, variables are measures of association (eta for the dichotomous categorical variables and Pearson's r for the timing and counting variables). For convenience and simplicity, significant positive and negative relationships are referred to as the effect of the executional variable on the dependent variables, but the reader is cautioned that this is not the only interpretation. An alternative interpretation is that the executional variable just happens to be present in a set of commercials exhibiting significantly higher or lower recall, comprehension, or persuasion scores. The executional variable may be causing, or contributing to, the effect, or it may be merely a correlate of other variables that are actually the active agents in the relationship.

The remainder of this chapter is organized according to the pattern of relationships with the three dependent variables (for example, variables affecting all three positively, all three negatively, or recall and comprehension only). The rationale for this organization is that there should be a common thread to the explanation of variables performing in a similar pattern.

Variables Positively Affecting Recall, Comprehension, and Persuasion

Of the twenty-six variables relating to the information content of the commercials, only convenience of use had a significantly positive effect on all three dependent variables (table 5–1). In fact, the general relationship between amount of specific information and commercial recall and comprehension was negative.

When the brand name reinforces the intended use of the product, recall, comprehension, and persuasion are higher. This is also true when the commercial claims its product has a particular feature or performance attribute that no other product can claim. This relationship between claiming something unique for the product and commercial performance is consistent with the most fundamental models of advertising practice. Further discussion of this latter finding is presented in subsequent chapters.

When the first 10 seconds of the commercial create suspense, questions, surprise, drama, or something that otherwise gains attention, the effect seems to carry through to all three performance measures. This finding is contrary to the finding by McEwen and Leavitt (1976) that opening suspense was negatively related to recall. In the McEwen and Leavitt study, however, opening suspense was confounded with a late identification of the product, a source of confounding not in the present data.

Demonstration of the product either by showing how it is used, how it works, or the results of use has a positive effect on recall, key message comprehension, and persuasion. This finding is consistent with the conclusion of a body of research on the positive effects of product demonstrations in television commercials (McEwen and Leavitt 1976; Ogilvy and Raphaelson 1982; Burke Marketing Research 1978).

The amount of time that the product (not just the package) is visible on the screen also appears to be important. And, in general, commercials with live action (finished or unfinished) score higher than storyboards.

Variables Negatively Affecting Recall, Comprehension, and Persuasion

Information about product components and ingredients or a major focus on something about how the product is made seemed to have a definite dampening effect on the commercial's performance (table 5–2). The issue is probably

Table 5–1
Variables Positively Affecting Recall, Comprehension, and Persuasion

	Recall	Comprehension	Persuasion
Information content			
Convenience of use	[+]	[+]	[+]
Congruence of commercial elements			
Brand name reinforces product use	+	[+]	[+]
Promises, appeals, propositions			
Brand-differentiating claim	[+]	[+]	[+]
Commercial structure			
Opening surprise/suspense	(+)	[+]	+
Commercial format			
Demonstration of product in use	[+]	[+]	[+]
Demonstration of results of use	[+]	[+]	[+]
Timing and counting variables			
Seconds actual product is on screen	[+]	[+]	[+]
Commercial finish			
Live action	[+]	[+]	[+]

[+] = 95 percent significance level; + = 90 percent significance level.

Table 5–2
Variables Negatively Affecting Recall, Comprehension, and Persuasion

	Recall	Comprehension	Persuasion
Information content			
Components/ingredients	[−]	[−]	[−]
Nutrition/health	[−]	[−]	[−]
Promises, appeals, propositions			
Attributes/ingredients major focus	[−]	[−]	−
Commercial tone or atmosphere			
Conservative/traditional	[−]	−	−
Commercial characters			
Male principal character	−	[−]	[−]

[−] = 95 percent significance level; − = 90 percent significance level.

not whether commercials should try to communicate this type of information but whether it can be communicated in a more interesting manner and whether it can be made clearly relevant to what the prospective consumer wants to know about the product. Information on nutrition and health also had a negative effect on overall commercial performance. This finding is consistent with other research findings that consumers do not normally understand or use nutrition information (Jacoby, Chestnut, and Silberman 1977).

Commercials that convey a conservative or traditional tone were also less likely to be effective, as were commercials with a male principal character.

The effect of the latter of these variables may be due to the fact that many of the commercials tested were for products bought primarily by women for use in the household.

Variables Affecting Recall and/or Comprehension but Not Persuasion

Information on results of using the product (for example, bouncy hair, feeling healthier, will not yellow floors) had a positive effect on key message comprehension but did not necessarily improve overall recall of the commercial (table 5–3). In contrast, commercials referring to user's satisfaction, preference for the brand, or length of time the consumer has used the advertised product appeared to have a negative impact on both recall and comprehension. This finding is contrary to prior findings that have tended to support the effects of customer testimonials on recall (for example, Burke Marketing Research 1978). This may be the result of so many commercials making user satisfaction claims that they have lost interest and credibility with the audience.

Total information content of the commercial is predictably negatively related to recall and comprehension. When commercials try to communicate a variety of information, their recall and comprehension scores suffer. Contrary to the conclusion of numerous other studies that television commercials carry little information (Bauer and Greyser 1968, Resnik and Stern 1977), these findings indicate a high level of information content. The problem is that greater information content had a dampening effect on recall and comprehension.

When commercials identified the manufacturer or distributor of the product, they got the key message across to the audience, but they did not necessarily improve recall of the commercial. Visual brand sign-off at the end of the commercial (brand name, package, or other obvious identifier) increased recall.

When the setting in the commercial was directly related to where the product will be used or where it is purchased, related recall and key message comprehension were positively affected. When the setting was unrelated to product use but was somehow relevant to product performance, key message comprehension in particular suffered. A relevant but unrelated setting would be a watch strapped to the bottom of a speedboat to demonstrate water and shock resistance. The apparent effect of these unusual settings is to impede rather than facilitate key message comprehension.

Setting was measured a second time to establish whether it was indoors, outdoors, or in a neutral setting (that is, not apparent where it was). When the setting was indoors, key message comprehension was higher. This finding is consistent with the positive effect of directly related settings since most of

Table 5–3
Variables Affecting Recall and/or Comprehension but Not Persuasion

	Recall	Comprehension
Information content		
Results of using		[+]
User satisfaction	–	[–]
Total information (sum of twenty-six information variables)	[–]	[–]
Brand/product identification		
Manufacturer/distributor idenfied		[+]
Visual brand sign-off	[+]	
Congruence of commercial elements		
Setting relevant to product performance, not use		[–]
Setting directly related to where product used	[+]	[+]
Visual devices		
Graphic displays/charts	[–]	[–]
Substantive supers	[–]	–
Auditory devices		
Memorable rhyme/Mnemonic	[+]	+
Promises, appeals, propositions		
Product performance major focus	–	[+]
Commercial tone or atmosphere		
Cute/adorable		[+]
Humorous	[+]	[+]
Comparisons		
Direct comparisons/naming competitor(s)	[–]	[–]
Unsubstantiated claims (e.g., puffery)	[+]	[+]
Commercial format		
Fantasy/surrealism dominant	[+]	
Commercial characters		
Female principal character	[–]	
Child/infant principal character[a]	[+]	+
Animal principal character[a]	[+]	–
Animated cartoon principal character	[+]	
Commercial setting		
Indoors		[+]
No setting	[–]	[–]
Timing and counting variables		
Length of commercial	[+]	[+]
Times brand name mentioned	[+]	
Seconds until product category identification	[–]	
Seconds until brand name identification	[–]	
Seconds until product/package shown	[–]	
Times brand name/logo on screen	[+]	

[+] or [–] = 95 percent significance level; + or – = 90 percent significance level.

[a]The children and animal principal character variables occur primarily in only two product categories so care should be exercised in interpreting these findings.

the products in the database were household products for indoor use. When there was no setting, recall was lower.

Visual devices such as charts and superscripts on the screen had a negative effect on recall and comprehension. Although these devices are designed to support and reinforce relevant parts of the message, they may appear to be impediments. The presence of on-screen charts and supers may also be merely a correlate of product information that is difficult to communicate, and their presence may just contribute to the overload of information. The real issue is that graphs, charts, and supers appeared to be unhelpful in communicating this information. This finding is contrary to the conclusion in prior research that supers may improve the commercial's performance (Ogilvy and Raphaelson 1982). However, earlier findings have referred to supers that reinforce the key message, while results of the present study apply to superscripts in general. Rhymes and mnemonic devices, like slogans, had a positive effect on both recall and comprehension. This finding is consistent with previous research.

When a major focus of the commercial was to communicate what the product does (lasts longer, is more comfortable, makes teeth whiter), key message comprehension was positively affected, but general recall of the commercial was negatively affected. This was a paradoxical finding. Emphasis on product performance as the key message was apparently associated with commercials that in general are not particularly memorable.

Commercials that convey either a cute-adorable or humorous feeling in general performed better on recall and comprehension. However, they were not systematically effective at inducing people to try the product.

Direct comparisons in which competitors were named seem to have a negative impact on recall and comprehension, but unsubstantiated puffed-up claims of superiority (product declared best, finest, and so on without identification of dimension or attribute) had positive effects on both recall and key message comprehension. It is doubtful that prospective consumers find the puffed claims more convincing since persuasion was not affected, but they may appreciate the simplicity of the communication compared to more complex direct comparisons. The more important issue is that neither puffery nor direct comparisons appear to be particularly persuasive.

When a child, animal, or animated cartoon was the principal character, recall was positively affected. In contrast, when an adult female was the principal character, the commercials were less memorable. Apparently, predominantly female audiences find female principal characters less memorable.

Long commercials received higher recall and comprehension scores. When the number of times the brand name is mentioned in the commercial was above average, related recall increased. The brand name was mentioned an average of four times in a 30-second commercial. The same was true for the number of times the brand name or logo was shown on the screen (average for 30 seconds is four). The number of seconds before the commercial identifies the product category or brand name or shows the product or package was negatively related to recall. When the commercial takes too long to identify the product category (average for 30-second commercial is 5 to 7 seconds), recall of the commercial suffers.

Variables Affecting Persuasion Only

Only two executional variables had an effect on persuasion without also having an impact on recall or comprehension (table 5–4). When the tone or feeling of the commercial is relaxed and comfortable, persuasion is positively affected but not necessarily recall or comprehension.

The same is true for comparisons between the advertised product and an unnamed competitor or competitors. The process at work here is probably similar to the effect of an explicit brand-differentiating claim. Indirect comparisons imply a differentiating characteristic without necessarily claiming specifically that it is the only product that can make this claim. Indirect comparisons do not identify a specific competitor but may induce prospects to try a product that appears to be claiming something different.

Variables Affecting Recall and Persuasion but Not Comprehension

Sensory information positively affected recall and persuasion but not necessarily key message comprehension (table 5–5). This is probably more of a definitional problem than a statement of how sensory information works in a commercial. How the product tastes, smells, and feels may not frequently be part of the specified key message, although these findings suggest that it probably should be.

Information about new products or new features of established products appeared to affect recall negatively, while it positively affected persuasion. This is consistent with the general negative effects found for most informa-

Table 5–4
Variables Affecting Persuasion Only

	Persuasion
Commercial tone or atmosphere	
Relaxed/comfortable	[+]
Comparisons	
Indirect comparisons with unnamed competition	[+]

[+] = 95 percent significance level.

Table 5–5
Variables Affecting Recall and Persuasion but Not Comprehension

	Recall	*Persuasion*
Information content		
Sensory (taste, smell, and so on)	[+]	[+]
New product or new features	–	[+]
Commercial format		
Continuity of action	+	[+]
Commercial characters		
Actor playing role of principal character	[–]	[+]
No principal character	[–]	[+]
Commercial setting		
Outdoors	+	[–]
Promises, appeals, propositions		
Total propositions	[–]	[–]

[+] or [–] = 95 percent significance level; + or – = 90 percent significance level.

tion content on recall and the positive effects on persuasion of claiming something unique. The reason comprehension is not negatively affected is probably again largely definitional. While related recall was lower because of the greater information load and lack of prior familiarity with the new product, what was recalled (for example, what is new about the product) was the advertiser's key message.

Continuity of action—or a single storyline throughout the commercial—positively affected recall and persuasion. The finding for recall is supported by prior studies—notably, McEwen and Leavitt (1976). Given the positive effect on persuasion, continuity of the commercial storyline is an important factor in commercial effectiveness.

Actors playing the role of the principal character and having principal characters on screen (versus voice-over only) both had paradoxical effects. Both affected persuasion positively but affected recall negatively. The effect of no principal character is easier to explain. When there is no principal character, there is less about the commercial to recall, and the absence of a principal on-screen character indicates that more time is probably devoted to the product. When this happens, respondents may be more likely to want to try the product but have difficulty remembering the commercial. The effect of actors as principal on-screen characters is harder to explain. Female principal character, male principal character, and actor playing role of principal character are the three most frequently occurring types of on-camera characters (61, 54, and 45 percent of all commercials respectively). All are negatively related to recall, and their ubiquity may be the principal cause. No general type of character occurring in more than 15 percent of all commercials had a positive effect on recall.

When the commercial setting was outdoors, recall was higher, but persuation was lower. This effect on persuasion is consistent with other findings for relevance of the setting to actual usage or purchase situations. Since most of the products in the database are for use in household, outdoor commercial settings are unique and perhaps more distinctive (hence, higher recall) but less directly relevant to how and where the product is to be used (hence, lower persuasion).

The total number of different appeals in the commercial is negatively related to recall and persuasion. This finding is consistent with the general negative effects of information load on recall found in this study and with the effects of message confusion in prior studies (McEwen and Leavitt 1976).

Variables Affecting Comprehension and Persuasion but Not Recall

All relationships involving comprehension and persuasion were either both positive or both negative (table 5–6). For example, when the product was double-branded, identifying either the producer or a family of brands, key message comprehension and persuasion were positively affected. However, this does not mean that the commercial is particularly memorable.

The total number of different appeals that the commercial attempted to communicate (for example, sexual, comfort, safety, social approval) was negatively related to comprehension and persuasion. This is probably a manifestation of general information overload and confusion, but in this case it does not necessarily mean that the commercial was less memorable, just that the key message was harder to pick out as well as a particular reason for trying the product.

The total number of on-screen characters and the presence of a background cast in the commercial also appeared to have a dampening effect

Table 5–6
Variables Affecting Comprehension and Persuasion but Not Recall

	Recall	Persuasion
Brand/product identification		
Family-branded product	+	[+]
Promises, appeals, propositions		
Total appeals (sum of nine variables)	[−]	[−]
Commercial characters		
Background cast	[−]	[−]
Timing and counting variables		
Number of on-screen characters	[−]	[−]

[+] or [−] = 95 percent significance level; + or − = 90 percent significance level.

on comprehension and persuasion. While the presence of extra characters on screen does not affect recall of the commercial, their presence did seem to get in the way of key message comprehension and persuasion. A word of caution in interpreting this finding is that this relationship may change for specific advertisers. A separate validation study indicated that additional characters sometimes improves comprehension and persuasion. The appropriate caveat for this finding is that additional characters are only effective if their presence adds something to the key message communication; otherwise, they impede communication.

In fact, this caveat should be applied in interpreting all the findings in this study. General relationships for the entire database apply across many different commercials, advertisers, and products. They are general findings that must be applied with great caution to any specific commercial or advertiser.

6
Multivariate Analyses

Previous research on the effects of advertising execution has tended to be bivariate in nature. While such analyses are useful and, in some cases, the only practical form of analysis, they do not capture fully the relationships that may exist within a set of executional variables and measures of advertising performance. Bivariate analyses may not reveal important underlying constructs or potential redundancy among variables. The complexity of a large dataset often makes it difficult to comprehend larger relationships without employing data reduction methods. The analyses described in this chapter employ such data reduction techniques.

Factor Analysis of Executional Factors

A principal components analysis of executional factors was carried out using those items that appeared in at least 5 percent of the commercials and that attained a reliability of at least .60. Exceptions to this rule were made only when the inclusion of an item appeared to add to the interpretability of a particular factor. An analysis of variables occurring in at least 10 percent of the commercials produced a nearly identical solution, suggesting that the solution is relatively robust.

The dichotomous nature of many of the individual items necessitated a correction for differences in the marginal distribution of the items. This was accomplished by means of Holley's procedure (Holley and Guilford 1964). Twenty-four factors emerged in the analysis, accounting for 62 percent of the total variance among the executional items. Both the eigenvalues greater than 1 and the scree test suggested this number of factors. Varimax rotation and several oblique rotations of the factor structure matrix were carried out. The oblique rotations failed to add appreciably to the identification of simple structure, as measured by the hyperplane counts of the factors. Therefore, the varimax rotation was retained. Table 6–1 reports the composition of the obtained factors. Each of the factors appeared readily interpretable.

Table 6–1
Factor Structure of Advertising Executional Codes
(N = 1,059 commercials)

Factor 1: Relevant setting
No setting (– .89)
Indoor setting (.83)
Setting directly relevant to product purchase or use (.81)
Slice of life (.35)

Factor 2: Product benefits
Information on results of using product (.78)
Product performance or benefit is major appeal (.74)
Results of using product are demonstrated (.71)
Problem solution format (.65)
Sensory information (– .43)
Total appeals (.37)

Factor 3: Time until identification
Time until product category identification (.79)
Time until brand name identification (.84)
Time until product or package is shown (.79)
Principal message in first 10 seconds (.59)
Commercial length (.31)

Factor 4: Product attributes/components
Information on components, contents, or ingredients (.83)
Attributes or ingredients are major appeal (.81)
Information on nutrition or health (.61)
Total information (.54)
Total appeals (.52)
Conservative/traditional tone (.35)

Factor 5: Cast
Number of on-screen characters (.79)
Background cast (.77)
Outdoor setting (.61)
Slice of life (.43)
Male principal characters (.41)

Factor 6: Stills/storyboard/animation
Principal character animated (.79)
Stills/storyboard (.73)
Principal character(s) actor playing role of ordinary person (– .57)
Animation/cartoon/rotoscope (.56)
On-camera spokesperson (– .52)

Factor 7: Brand prominence
Time package is on screen (.81)
Time brand name or logo is on screen (.54)
Time actual product is on screen (.54)
Length of commercial (.52)
Times brand name or logo is on screen (.46)

Factor 8: Front-end impact
Front-end impact (.73)
Conservative/traditional tone (– .71)
Modern/contemporary tone (.61)
Puff/unsubstantiated claim (.56)

Table 6–1 (continued)

Factor 9: User satisfaction
Information on users' satisfaction/dedication/loyalty (.77)
Testimonial by product user (.73)
On-camera spokesperson (.34)

Factor 10: Emotional tone
Relaxed/comfortable tone (.69)
Total emotional tone (.60)
Warm and caring tone (.53)
Wholesome/healthy tone (.38)

Factor 11: Humor
Humorous tone (.72)
Cute/adorable tone (.70)
Total emotional tone (.46)
Principal character female (– .38)

Factor 12: Auditory Memory Devices
Music a major element (.68)
Memorable rhymes, slogans, or mnemonics (.63)
Music present (.41)

Factor 13: Company identification
Company manufacturing or distributing product is identified (.71)
Product is double branded (.69)
Brand name reinforces product benefit (.60)

Factor 14: Demonstration in use
Setting unrelated to product use but related to performance (– .69)
Demonstration of product in use (.56)
Setting directly relevant to product use or purchase (.36)
Enjoyment appeal (.30)

Factor 15: On-screen characters
No principal characters (– .78)
Principal character male (.41)
On-screen spokesperson (.38)
Principal character actor playing role (.35)
Principal character female (.34)
Use of visual memory device (– .34)

Factor 16: Continuity
Continuity of action (.80)
Number of vignettes (– .80)

Factor 17: Serious tone/graphic displays
Somber/serious tone (.77)
Graphic displays (.51)

Factor 18: Brand sign-off
Auditory brand sign-off (.73)
Visual brand sign-off (.71)

Factor 19: Indirect Comparison
Indirect comparison (.82)
Direct comparison (– .55)

Factor 20: Product reminder
Product reminder is major appeal (.70)
Total appeals (.58)

Table 6–1 (continued)

Factor 21: Convenience in use
Information on convenience in use (.76)
Superiority claim (− .39)
Direct comparison with other product (− .38)

Factor 22: Fantasy
Fantasy, exaggeration, or surrealism is a dominant element (.70)
Use of visual memory device (.42)
Animation/cartoon/rotoscope (.37)
Times brand name mentioned (− .30)

Factor 23: Research
Research results (.72)
Total information (.34)
Length of commercial (.30)

Factor 24: Substantive supers
Substantive supers (.72)
Superiority claim (.39)

Description of the Factors

Factor 1 is a bipolar factor related to the setting of the commercial. The negative pole of this factor is no setting—that is, a nondescript, unidentified setting. The positive pole of this factor is the use of a setting directly relevant to the purchase or use of the product being advertised. It is not surprising, given the nature of the products included in the dataset, that the settings most frequently related to product use or purchase are indoors.

Factor 2 is related to information about the benefits of using the product. This includes information about the results of using the product, product benefits as a major appeal, demonstrations of product results, and a problem and solution format. Information on the sensory aspects of a product are negatively related to this factor.

Factor 3 is related to the amount of time that elapses in the commercial before the product category or brand is identified. This tends to be relatively brief for most commercials, so message in the first 10 seconds is also positively related to this factor.

Factor 4 is related to presence of information on product attributes, ingredients, or components. Many commercials in the dataset are for food and drug products so it is not surprising that nutrition and health information are also related to this factor.

Factor 5 is related to the presence of a larger number of on-screen characters in the commercial. The relationship of an outdoor setting to this factor probably means only that more characters are likely to appear in outdoor settings. The modest relationship of male characters with this factor may also suggest that when a male is a principal character, it is likely to be in a situation involving other characters and/or an outdoor setting.

Factor 6 is a storyboard dimension. This factor reflects the use of animation in storyboards and animatic formats. As such, this factor confounds the use of animation and the use of a storyboard form of production. Analyses designed to examine the effects of each of these devices separately are reported in chapter 7.

Factor 7 is related to the amount of time devoted to the product, package, or other brand identifier during the commercial. For that reason, it was labeled brand prominence.

Factor 8 is associated with the use of devices designed to obtain attention by surprise or suspense at the beginning of the commercial. The evocation of a modern/contemporary tone, as opposed to a conservative/traditional tone, and the use of puffery are also associated with this factor. Front-end impact is one of several items used in this stage of the analysis that had not quite attained the desired interrater reliability criterion. Addition of this variable provides a better definition of the factor than was obtained by use of the other three items alone.

Factor 9 is related to information on the satisfaction and loyalty of product users. This factor is also defined by testimonials of product users and an on-camera spokesperson.

Factor 10 is related to the evocation of pleasant emotions such as relaxed/comfortable tone, warm and caring tone, and wholesome/healthy tone. The items loading this factor tend to be on the low side of acceptable reliability but appear to define an intuitively reasonable factor.

Factor 11 is related to the use of humor in a commercial. It is highly correlated with other items related to humor that did not attain sufficient frequency for inclusion in the analysis.

Factor 12 is related to the use of music to carry the primary commercial message and the use of memorable rhymes or mnemonics. These mnemonics and the use of music appear to be designed to facilitate recall of the commercial message. For this reason, the factor was named auditory memory devices.

Factor 13 is related to the identification of the company manufacturing the product and family branding. A brand name that reinforces the product's benefit is also related.

Unlike factor 2, which is related to the demonstration of the results of using a product, factor 14 is related to the demonstration of a product in use. It is also related to relevant setting and product enjoyment appeals.

Factor 15 is related to use of a primary on-screen character versus no on-screen characters. Commercials without characters may still employ a voice-over spokesperson to deliver the message, but that spokesperson is never seen.

Factor 16 is a message continuity factor. Commercials that score high on this factor have a clear beginning, middle, and end and do not use a vignette format. They tend to tell a single story from the beginning of the commercial to the end.

Factor 17 is associated with a somber, serious tone and the use of graphic displays. The item somber/serious is, in fact, related to a number of other items not included in the present analysis, including hard-sell tone and announcement format. These items were not included in the formal analysis because of their low frequency of occurrence in the dataset. When such items are included, the use of graphics separates into a different factor from serious/somber tone. Nevertheless, the factor as presented is intuitively acceptable since most commercials offering graphic displays, at least in the present dataset, appear to have a serious/somber tone.

Factor 18 is an uncomplicated factor related to auditory and visual brand sign-offs.

Factor 19 is a bipolar factor related to product comparisons. The stronger, positive pole is related to indirect comparisons that do not specifically name a competitor. The negative pole of the factor is related to the use of a direct comparison, naming competitors.

Factor 20 is related to product reminder as the major focus of the commercial and total number of different appeals. An earlier analysis produced a factor loaded exclusively by total appeals. The item product reminder as a major appeal was not included in this analysis because of its low reliability. Closer examination of the data suggested a reason for this low reliability. Product reminder was originally conceived as an item for use when there was no clearly identifiable product appeal—that is, no ingredient/attribute, performance, or psychological appeal. A number of commercials clearly fit this description, and there was good coder agreement on these commercials. The source of unreliability for this item appears to have been a large number of commercials that offer numerous appeals. In such cases it is not always clear whether any one should be considered a major appeal. Coders in such cases may either indicate no major appeal, product reminder, or multiple appeals. Since the presence of product reminder adds considerably to the meaning of the factor, this item was retained in the reported analysis.

Factor 21 is most strongly related to information on the convenience of using the advertised product. When a commercial claims product convenience, it appears less likely that the commercial will also make a product superiority claim or use a direct comparison format.

Factor 22 is primarily related to the use of fantasy, surrealism, or exaggeration in the commercial. It is also related to visual memory devices, animation, and a below-average number of brand name mentions. It is related to several items not reported in the present analysis because of their infrequency of occurrence, including unusual sound effects and a surreal tone.

Factor 23 is another factor where the addition of an otherwise infrequent or unreliable item provided assistance in interpreting the factor. Factor 23 is related to the total information content and the length of the commercial. Presentation of research results added to the interpretability of this factor.

Factor 24 is related to the use of substantive superscripts. Making a superiority claim is also related.

Relationship of Factors to Product Categories

Factor scores were computed for each commercial on all twenty-four factors. The use of the 5 percent frequency criterion tended to eliminate much of the confounding of executional items and product categories. An examination of the factor scores of each category revealed no serious confounding of factors and product categories. Although no complete confounding occurred, some differences were present. Hygiene products were more likely to score high on factor 2, product benefits and results of using. The over-the-counter remedies product category tended to be higher on factor 17 (serious tone/graphics) and factor 2 (product benefits, results of use). The cleaners, polishers category was high on factor 2 (product benefits) while all food-related product categories tended to be lower. The other household products category was high on factor 21 (convenience in use). Breakfast foods were somewhat more likely than other product categories to score high on factor 12 (auditory memory devices). Finally, the food categories were typically higher on factor 4 (ingredients and attributes). While category differences are present, no factors were confounded with any one category and did not pose a particular problem for further analyses.

Factor scores were computed for each factor using the entire matrix of factor (component) score coefficients. This method of computing factor scores has the advantage of maintaining the orthogonality of the factors in subsequent analyses. Factor scores computed using only the two or three items with the largest loadings for each factor produced results quite similar to those reported using the entire matrix.

The variable, brand-differentiating message, failed to load appreciably on any of the factors. Since both creative philosophies and the earlier bivariate analyses suggested it was an important variable related to recall, comprehension, and persuasion, it was included as a twenty-fifth factor in subsequent analyses. No other variables that appeared to be related to one of the performance measures in the bivariate analyses failed to load one of the other twenty-four factors. The set of twenty-five factors was then used as a set of independent variables in a series of regression analyses designed to predict each of the measures of advertising effectiveness.[1]

Table 6–2
Executional Factors Predicting Recall

	Multiple R	Beta[a]
Humor (factor 1)	.22	.21
Brand-differentiating message	.28	.20
Auditory memory device (factor 12)	.30	.12
On-screen characters (factor 15)	.31	−.08
Brand prominence (factor 7)	.32	.07
Product attributes/components (factor 4)	.33	−.08
Company identification (factor 13)	.34	−.07
Product benefits (factor 2)	.34	.07
Brand sign-off (factor 18)	.35	.06
Front-end impact (factor 8)	.35	.06
Convenience in use (factor 21)	.36	.06

Multiple R = .36
R^2 = .13
Adjusted R^2 = .12
[a]Standardized regression coefficients, all significant at the .05 level.

Multiple Regression Analyses

Table 6–2 reports the results of a stepwise regression analysis designed to predict related recall. The table reports results obtained after the recall measure was corrected for product category effects (the residual term described in chapter 4). Similar results were obtained with uncorrected recall scores, although the amount of variance accounted for was higher (20 percent as compared to 13 percent in the reported analysis) and several additional items entered the equation.

The reported analysis reveals that numerous factors related to either obtaining attention or facilitating memory are positively related to recall. Humor has the strongest relationship with recall, followed by brand-differentiating message. Humor has been found to be related to recall in previous research (Sternthal and Craig 1973). Other factors positively related to recall are use of auditory memory devices, length of time in the commercial devoted to the product (brand prominence), front-end impact, and brand sign-off. The negative relationship between on-screen characters and recall appears to result from the fact that many commercials without characters devote more time to the product and have a greater tendency to use memory devices. Brand-differentiating messages, product benefits, and information on convenience of use are positively related to recall. Information on product attri-

Table 6–3
Executional Factors Predicting Comprehension

	Multiple R	Beta[a]
Brand-differentiating message	.16	.17
Humor (factor 11)	.20	.11
Convenience in use (factor 21)	.22	.11
Auditory memory device (factor 12)	.24	.08
Front-end impact (factor 8)	.25	.08
Cast (factor 5)	.26	– .07
Time until identification (factor 3)	.27	.06

Multiple R = .27
R^2 = .06
Adjusted R^2 = .06
[a]Standardized regression coefficients, all significant at the .05 level.

butes, components, and ingredients is negatively related to recall, as is the company identification factor.

Relatively less of the variance in the comprehension measure could be accounted for by executional factors (table 6–3). Only 6 percent of the variance of the adjusted comprehension measure was shared with executional factors. An analysis of the unadjusted comprehension measure accounted for 14 percent of the variance but usually identified the same factors as were identified with the adjusted measures. The items positively related to comprehension are similar to those related to recall. This is not surprising given the correlation between recall and comprehension. As expected, brand-differentiating message is the single best predictor of key message comprehension. The definition of key message would tend to involve the brand-differentiating claim. Convenience in use is also positively related to comprehension. Again, this may be because convenience is frequently defined as the key selling message. As with recall, humor, use of an auditory memory device, and front-end impact are positively related to comprehension. The presence of a background cast and a storyboard format appear to have modest negative relationships with comprehension. A longer time until identification of the product or brand being advertised appears to be positively related to comprehension. This finding is contrary to expectations, and the relationship, while significant, is relatively minor. This may be an artifact related to the fact that longer commercials tend to take more time to identify the product or brand. Thus, the obtained effect may be due to a longer commercial, in which case this finding makes sense.

A separate analysis of the unadjusted comprehension measure (uncorrected for product category differences) identified numerous other factors related to comprehension. These additional factors could be defined as the key message of a commercial: product benefits, demonstration in use, research findings, attributes/ingredients, product reminder, and company identification. All these factors, except attributes/ingredients and product reminder, were positively related to comprehension. These executional variables also have the greatest probability of being specific to a particular product category. The attributes and ingredients factor is most likely to occur in commercials for over-the-counter products, cleaners and solvents, and beverages. Company identification is most likely to occur among household products and soft-hard goods. It is worth noting that while attributes/ingredients were negatively related to comprehension, they were positively related to comprehension in the beverages category, suggesting that the use of attribute/ingredient information is not uniformly negatively related to comprehension.

The persuasion measure may be examined in a number of ways. For example, certain product and brand characteristics that are captured by the Fair Share measure might be used as predictors along with the various executional factors. The persuasion measure, alternatively, may be corrected for category differences and only executional elements used for prediction. Finally, recall and comprehension could also be included as predictors under the assumption that a relationship exists between these two measures and persuasion. Each of these analyses is discussed separately.

It is not surprising that a strong relationship exists between the expected level of switching to a brand, represented by Fair Share, and the raw persuasion score. Table 6–4 describes this relationship. Some 72 percent of the variance in the raw persuasion measure is attributable to Fair Share. Brand-differentiating message is the strongest executional element related to raw

Table 6–4
Executional and Product Factors Predicting Raw Persuasion

	Multiple R	*Beta*[a]
Fair Share	.85	.83
Brand-differentiating message	.86	.11
Cast (factor 5)	.86	− .05
Front-end impact (factor 8)	.86	.04
Auditory memory device (factor 12)	.86	.04
Continuity (factor 16)	.86	.03

Multiple R = .86
R^2 = .75
Adjusted R^2 = .74
[a]Standardized regression coefficients, all significant at the .05 level.

Table 6-5
**Executional Factors Predicting Persuasion, Corrected for
Product Category Effect**

	Multiple R	*Beta*[a]
Brand-differentiating message	.23	.22
Product reminder (factor 20)	.25	–.10
Convenience in use (factor 21)	.27	.09
Animatics/storyboard (factor 6)	.28	–.09
Company identification (factor 13)	.29	.07
Cast (factor 5)	.30	–.06
Continuity (factor 16)	.31	.06
Research (factor 23)	.31	.06
Serious/graphics (factor 17)	.32	–.06

Multiple R = .32
R^2 = .10
Adjusted R^2 = .09
[a]Standardized regression coefficients, all significant at the .05 level.

persuasion. The presence of a background cast is negatively related to raw persuasion, while front-end impact, use of auditory memory devices, and continuity are positively related.

Different executional factors emerge as significant predictors of persuasion once it has been adjusted for product category effects. As shown in table 6-5, brand-differentiating message is still the most important predictor, accounting for about 4 percent of the total variance in the adjusted persuasion measure. Nine executional variables account for roughly 10 percent of the total variance of the corrected persuasion measure. Some of the observed differences may be attributable to differences in the levels of recall and comprehension. In the analysis presented in table 6-6, recall and comprehension are included as independent variables. These results resemble those in table 6-4. Table 6-7 summarizes the findings of the regression analyses. This table may be contrasted with table 6-8, which summarizes the simple Pearson product moment correlation coefficients between the three measures of advertising performance and the executional factors.

One problem with the results of the regression analyses is that they treat each of the measures of advertising performance as if they were independent of each other. Recall and comprehension are highly correlated, while persuasion has a more modest, but significant, relationship with both recall and comprehension. When dependent measures like those in the previous analyses are related, it is often helpful to examine the relationships of the dependent measures simultaneously with the analysis of relationships between the inde-

Table 6–6
Executional, Product, and Performance Factors Predicting Raw Persuasion

	Multiple R	Beta[a]
Fair Share	.85	.77
Comprehension	.87	.10
Brand-differentiating message	.88	.08
Recall	.88	.11
Cast (factor 5)	.88	− .07
On-screen characters (factor 15)	.88	− .04
Front-end impact (factor 8)	.88	.03
Product attributes/components (factor 4)	.88	− .03

Multiple R = .88
R^2 = .77
Adjusted R^2 = .76
[a]Standardized regression coefficients, all significant at the .05 level.

Table 6–7
Summary of Relationship between Executional Factors and Measures of Advertising Performance

	Recall	Comprehension	Persuasion[b]
Brand-differentiating message	+ [a]	+	+
Humor (factor 11)	+	+	0
Front-end impact (factor 8)	+	+	0(−)
Auditory memory device (factor 12)	+	+	0
Cast (factor 5)	0	−	−
Convenience in use (factor 21)	+	+	+
Storyboard (factor 6)	0	−	−
On-screen characters (factor 15)	−	0	0(−)
Brand prominence (factor 7)	+	0	0
Brand sign-off (factor 18)	+	0	0
Product attributes/components (factor 4)	−	0	0(−)
Research (factor 23)	0	0	+
Product benefits (factor 2)	+	0	+
Continuity (factor 16)	0	0	+
Company identification (factor 13)	−	0	−
Product reminder (factor 20)	0	0	−
Time until identification (factor 3)	0	+	0

[a]Key: + means significant positive relationship observed; − means significant negative relationship observed; 0 means no significant relationship observed.
[b]Relationships noted in parentheses appeared only when raw persuasion was the dependent measure and Fair Share was one of the independent measures.

Table 6–8
Pearson Product Moment Correlations between Executional Factors and Measures of Advertising Performance for All Commercials

	Recall	*Comprehension*	*Persuasion*
Relevant setting (factor 1)	.07	.08	– .00
Product benefits (factor 2)	.03	.10	.03
Time until identification (factor 3)	– .08	– .00	– .04
Product attributes/components (factor 4)	– .13	– .12	– .09
Cast (factor 5)	– .02	– .12	– .15
Stills/storyboard (factor 6)	.09	– .05	– .05
Brand prominence (factor 7)	.08	.05	.03
Front-end impact (factor 8)	.07	.08	.06
User satisfaction (factor 9)	– .06	– .06	– .03
Emotional tone (factor 10)	– .05	– .07	.00
Humor (factor 11)	.24	.11	.05
Auditory memory devices (factor 12)	.14	.07	.02
Company identification (factor 13)	– .02	.08	.06
Demonstration in use (factor 14)	.06	.04	.04
On-screen characters (factor 15)	.06	.00	– .03
Continuity (factor 16)	.07	.04	.09
Serious/graphics (factor 17)	– .08	– .04	– .05
Brand sign-off (factor 18)	.08	.05	.01
Indirect comparisons (factor 19)	.03	.01	.04
Product reminder (factor 20)	– .03	– .08	– .08
Convenience in use (factor 21)	.11	.15	.05
Fantasy (factor 22)	.03	– .01	– .02
Research (factor 23)	– .03	– .06	.04
Substantive supers (factor 24)	.01	.01	.03
Brand-differentiating message	.15	.16	.23

pendent variables and dependent variables. This is what the following canonical analysis does.

Canonical Variate Analysis

A canonical analysis provides the opportunity to examine the relationships between two sets of data. In the present analysis these are the sets of executional factors and advertising effectiveness measures. Three significant canonical variates emerged from the analysis. Table 6–9 provides the load-

Table 6–9
Canonical Variate Analysis of Advertising Executional Factors and
Advertising Performance Measures (Adjusted for Product Category
Differences) for All Products
(N = 1,059)

	Canonical Variate 1	Canonical Variate 2	Canonical Variate 3
Recall	.97	.08	.23
Comprehension	.53	.57	.63
Persuasion	.37	.81	−.46
Relevant setting (factor 1)	.05	−.11	.26
Product benefits (factor 2)	.16	−.07	.19
Time until identification (factor 3)	−.08	.14	.32
Product attributes/components (factor 4)	−.16	−.04	.03
Cast (factor 5)	−.01	−.46	−.05
Storyboard/animatics (factor 6)	.16	−.45	−.18
Brand prominence (factor 7)	.24	.04	−.02
Front-end impact (factor 8)	.12	.16	.13
User satisfaction (factor 9)	−.15	−.06	−.07
Emotional tone (factor 10)	−.09	.11	−.23
Humor (factor 11)	.58	−.09	.13
Auditory memory devices (factor 12)	.24	−.06	.20
Company identification (factor 13)	−.21	.32	.23
Demonstration in use (factor 14)	−.10	.08	−.09
On-screen characters (factor 15)	.20	−.17	.07
Continuity (factor 16)	.16	.16	−.25
Serious/graphics (factor 17)	.05	−.06	.11
Brand sign-off (factor 18)	.17	−.05	.10
Indirect comparison (factor 19)	.01	.05	−.18
Product reminder (factor 20)	.08	−.28	−.10
Convenience in use (factor 21)	.03	.11	.50
Fantasy (factor 22)	.10	−.13	−.03
Research (factor 23)	.01	.11	−.38
Substantive supers (factor 24)	.08	.12	−.03
Brand-differentiating message	.48	.56	−.32

ings of each member of the two sets of variables on the three canonical variates.

Canonical variate 1 is strongly related to the recall measure, with a moderate comprehension component and a small persuasion component. As expected from previous analyses, the executional variable side of this composite variate tends to be most heavily loaded by humor and the presence of a brand-differentiating message. Other executional devices related to attention and memory processes also load this variate: brand prominence and use of auditory memory devices. Presence of information on product attributes/components, time until identification, emotional tone, cast, user satisfaction, demonstration in use, and company identification exhibit negative relationships with the recall variate. The interpretation of this variate is related to underlying memory processes. Executional factors that facilitate either attention to a commercial or retention of the commercial are related to the variate.

The second variate has a strong persuasion component with a moderate contribution from the comprehension measure. This variate is relatively independent of the recall measure. Brand-differentiating message and company identification are the strongest executional factors contributing positively to this variate. Factors contributing negatively are cast of characters, storyboard, and product reminder appeals.

Variate 3 is the most difficult to interpret. There is a relatively strong comprehension component and a negative persuasion component. Convenience in use, time until product identification, relevant setting, and company identification are the most positive contributing executional factors. Negative contributors are research results, brand-differentiating message, continuity of action, and emotional tone. This complex set of executional relationships appears to define a composite variable in which commercials affect comprehension without persuading prospective users.

Interaction Effects

Including interaction terms among factors identified by the factor analysis in the regression analyses sheds some light on the interpretation of variate 3. Commercials emphasizing convenience in the absence of a brand-differentiating message scored significantly higher on comprehension but significantly lower on persuasion. Since both convenience in use and brand-differentiating message are independently positively related to persuasion and convenience in use is not associated with a brand-differentiating message, it appears to have an inverse effect on persuasion. This would help to explain the positive loading of convenience in use and the negative loading of brand-differentiating message on the third canonical variate, defined as comprehension without persuasion. No other significant interaction effects among factors were identified.

Notes

1. The regression analyses reported throughout the remainder of the text are forward stepwise regressions, unless otherwise noted. Backward stepwise procedures

produce results quite similar to those reported. Since the factor scores are orthogonal, multicollinearity was not a problem and results tended to be quite stable regardless of the order of entry of the twenty-five variables. Unless otherwise noted, the dependent variables are residual scores computed by removing product category effects from the original measures of advertising effectiveness.

7
Analysis of Factors Moderating Relationships between Advertising Execution and Measures of Effectiveness

Product Life Cycle: New versus Established Products

Message factors influencing the memorability and persuasiveness of television commercials may differ for new and established products because established products have achieved high levels of consumer awareness and experience. By virtue of being novel, new product commercials may be more likely to induce trial usage. In the present study, a product was considered new if the commercial states that it was new, improved, or an extension of a product line. Of the 471 commercials coded as being for new or improved products, 400 were for new products, 60 were for line extensions, and 11 were for improved versions of established products.

In the previous chapter, predictions of recall, comprehension, and persuasion were carried out using the full set of 1,059 commercials. To examine differences between new and established products, these same analyses were carried out separately for the two subsets of commercials for new and non-new products. Table 7–1 provides the simple Pearson product moment correlations between the executional factors and the three measures of advertising effectiveness. In general, factors related more positively to recall or comprehension of new product commercials were humor, auditory memory devices, demonstration of the product in use, brand prominence, and user satisfaction. Factors more positively related to recall and comprehension for established products were emphasis on product benefits and brand differentiation. Factors more positively related to new product persuasion were relevant setting, brand prominence, auditory memory devices, and convenience of the product in use. Factors related more positively to established product persuasion were indirect comparisons (not naming competitors), substantive supers, and brand differentiation.

The emphasis on product benefits increased the memorability of estab-

Table 7–1
Pearson Product Moment Correlations between Executional Factors and Measures of Advertising Effectiveness for New/Improved versus Established Products

	Recall		Comprehension		Persuasion	
	New	Estab- lished	New	Estab- lished	New	Estab- lished
Relevant setting (factor 1)	.06	.08	.12	.04	.06	− .08
Product benefits (factor 2)	− .01	.10	.01	.22	− .00	.00
Time until identification (factor 3)	− .08	− .07	− .08	− .07	− .07	− .01
Product attributes/ingredients (factor 4)	− .14	− .13	− .14	− .14	− .21	− .03
Cast (factor 5)	− .03	− .01	− .14	− .10	− .13	− .13
Storyboard/animatics (factor 6)	− .13	.10	.08	− .01	− .08	.01
Brand prominence (factor 7)	.13	.08	.14	− .02	.09	− .07
Front-end impact (factor 8)	.09	.08	.08	.10	.07	.05
User satisfaction (factor 9)	.02	− .15	.06	− .17	.04	− .08
Emotional tone (factor 10)	− .05	− .02	− .08	− .04	.04	− .01
Humor (factor 11)	.24	.23	.12	.10	.02	.08
Auditory memory devices (factor 12)	.20	.08	.11	.00	.11	− .01
Company identification (factor 13)	− .03	− .03	.11	.04	.05	.06
Demonstration in use (factor 14)	.27	− .02	.07	− .02	.04	.04
On-screen characters (factor 15)	.09	.03	.02	− .02	− .03	− .06
Continuity (factor 16)	.08	.08	.07	.03	.11	.06
Serious/graphics (factor 17)	− .00	− .07	− .06	− .02	− .08	.01
Brand sign-off (factor 18)	.03	.10	.06	.02	.00	− .01
Indirect comparison (factor 19)	.01	.05	− .01	.01	− .04	.13
Product reminder (factor 20)	− .06	− .01	− .10	− .08	− .07	− .11
Convenience in use (factor 21)	.17	.06	.18	.14	.11	− .06
Fantasy (factor 22)	.04	.02	.04	− .04	− .05	.04
Research (factor 23)	− .04	− .02	− .01	− .09	.01	.02
Substantive supers (factor 24)	.00	.01	.03	− .03	− .02	.08
Brand-differentiating message	.12	.22	.18	.16	.16	.32

lished product commercials but had no apparent effect on new products. Relevant setting had a positive effect on all three performance measures for new products but had an apparent negative effect on persuasion for established products, which may need greater novelty in the setting and suggested application to induce trial. New products seemed to benefit more than established products from brand prominence in the commercial (repetition, time product is on screen). While user satisfaction had little effect for new products, it had a definite negative impact for established products. Auditory memory devices had a definite positive effect on commercials for new products—especially on recall—but they had no apparent effect on comprehension or persuasion for established products. Demonstration of the product in use had a significantly more positive effect on recall and comprehension of new product commercials but had about the same effect on persuasion for both new and established products. Indirect comparison worked best at inducing trial for established products. Information on convenience of the product in use affected new product persuasion positively but established product persuasion negatively. Product differentiation had a significant positive effect on all measures for both new and established products, but its impact was even more pronounced for established products.

Simple association measures provide limited insight into the strength of prediction. More appropriate for prediction is multiple regression analysis. Executional factors were used to predict each of the three effectiveness measures for new products and established products. Tables 7–2 and 7–3 are the results of the regression analyses predicting recall for new and established products respectively. Both equations predict roughly the same amount of the variance of the related recall measure. Three items are significant predictors in both analyses: brand-differentiating message, humor, and auditory memory devices. These items account for slightly more than 9 percent of the

Table 7–2
Prediction of Recall of New Product Commercials

	Multiple R	*Beta*[a]
Humor (factor 11)	.22	.22
Auditory memory devices (factor 12)	.29	.16
Brand-differentiating message	.31	.15
Brand prominence (factor 7)	.34	.12
On-screen characters (factor 15)	.36	.11
Convenience in use (factor 21)	.37	.12
Front-end impact (factor 8)	.39	.09

Multiple R = .39
R^2 = .15
Adjusted R^2 = .14
[a]Standardized regression coefficients, all significant at the .05 level.

Table 7–3
Prediction of Recall of Established Product Commercials

	Multiple R	Beta[a]
Brand-differentiating message	.24	.24
Humor (factor 11)	.30	.20
Product benefits (factor 2)	.34	.17
User satisfaction (factor 9)	.37	−.12
Brand sign-off (factor 18)	.38	.10
Product attributes/ingredients (factor 4)	.39	−.09
Auditory memory devices (factor 12)	.40	.09
Company identification (factor 13)	.41	−.09

Multiple R = .41
R^2 = .17
Adjusted R^2 = .16
[a]Standardized regression coefficients, all significant at the .05 level.

variance in recall in both datasets, although the order in which they enter the equations is different.

With the exception of two factors in the new product equation (brand-differentiating message and convenience in use), all other factors are related either to capturing viewer attention (humor, auditory devices, on-screen characters, front-end impact) or a longer focus on the product within the commercial (brand prominence). The relationship of the factors predicting recall for established products is more complex. Factors affecting established product recall negatively are user satisfaction, product attributes/ingredients, and company identification. Positive predictors, in addition to the three factors in common with new products, are product benefits and brand sign-off. The differences between predictors of recall for new and established products appear to be the greater importance of attention and memory-related devices for new products versus more complex message and benefit-oriented factors for established products.

This same attention/memory versus product message/benefit pattern emerged in the analyses of key message comprehension. This pattern is not surprising given the high correlation between the recall and comprehension measures. Roughly 12 percent of the variance in comprehension was accounted for in both new and established product commercial performance. Tables 7–4 and 7–5 provide details of these analyses. Brand-differentiating message is the best predictor of comprehension, accounting for about 3 percent of the variation in new and established product comprehension. Humor is the only other factor common to both. The time the product is on the screen (brand prominence) is a significant predictor of comprehension for

Table 7–4
Prediction of Comprehension of New Product Commercials

	Multiple R	Beta[a]
Brand-differentiating message	.17	.19
Convenience in use (factor 21)	.24	.16
Auditory memory device (factor 12)	.28	.15
Brand prominence (factor 7)	.31	.13
Humor (factor 11)	.34	.13
Front-end impact (factor 8)	.36	.11

Multiple R = .36
R^2 = .13
Adjusted R^2 = .12
[a]Standardized regression coefficients, all significant at the .05 level.

Table 7–5
Prediction of Comprehension of Established Product Commercials

	Multiple R	Beta[a]
Brand-differentiating message	.17	.17
Product benefits (factor 2)	.24	.17
User satisfaction (factor 9)	.28	− .15
Time until identification (factor 3)	.30	.13
Humor (factor 11)	.32	.11
Storyboard/animatics (factor 6)	.34	− .11

Multiple R = .34
R^2 = .12
Adjusted R^2 = .11
[a]Standardized regression coefficients, all significant at the .05 level.

new products but not for established products. Longer time to identification of the brand and product category is related to higher comprehension for established products. This result is related to the fact that longer commercials tended to take longer to identify the brand or product category. Thus, this finding may more reasonably be interpreted as suggesting that a longer commercial enhances comprehension.

Tables 7–6 and 7–7 provide details of the analysis for persuasion. The greatest differences between new and established products emerge in the prediction of the persuasion measure. Brand-differentiating claim is the only factor common to predicting both new and established product performance. It is the best predictor of persuasion for established products, accounting for over 8 percent of the total variance, but it is less important for new products,

Table 7–6
Prediction of Persuasion for New Product Commercials

	Multiple R	Beta[a]
Product attributes/components (factor 4)	.13	– .12
Company identification (factor 13)	.18	.12
Convenience in use (factor 21)	.22	.14
Brand-differentiating message	.25	.12
Serious/graphics (factor 17)	.27	– .10
Continuity (factor 16)	.28	.09
Brand prominence (factor 7)	.30	.09

Multiple R = .30
R^2 = .09
Adjusted R^2 = .07
[a]Standardized regression coefficients, all significant at the .05 level.

Table 7–7
Prediction of Persuasion for Established Product Commercials

	Multiple R	Beta[a]
Brand-differentiating message	.28	.26
Storyboard/animatics (factor 6)	.35	– .20
Product reminder (factor 20)	.37	– .12
Relevant setting (factor 1)	.39	– .12
User satisfaction (factor 9)	.41	– .12

Multiple R = .41
R^2 = .17
Adjusted R^2 = .16
[a]Standardized regression coefficients, all significant at the .05 level.

accounting for only about 1 percent of total variance. Executional factors account for over twice the variance in persuasion for established products (16 percent) than for new products (7 percent), but the influence of most of the executional factors on established product persuasion is negative.

Only brand-differentiating message is a significant positive predictor of persuasion for established brands. All other factors are negatively associated: storyboard/animatics, product reminder, relevant setting, and user satisfaction.

For new products, all but two factors, product attributes/components and serious tone/graphics, are positively related to the persuasion measure.

Company identification, convenience in use, brand-differentiating message, continuity of action, and brand prominence are significant positive predictors of new product persuasion. The first three represent potential reasons a consumer might purchase a new product, and the remaining two are factors that facilitate message effectiveness and ease of communication.

Care must be exercised when interpreting stepwise regression analyses like those reported here. Large numbers of observations, error of measurement, the fact that the three performance measures are related, and the tendency for stepwise procedures to identify small, chance differences may introduce spurious results. Additional clarification of the differences between new and established products is revealed by the use of canonical variate analysis.

Tables 7–8 and 7–9 are the results of the two canonical variate analyses. Three significant canonical variates emerged from the analysis of the established product commercials and two for new product commercials. The nature of the relationships in the two analyses is different and reinforces the findings from the regression analyses. The first canonical variate for the new product commercials is strongly related to recall and comprehension and is moderately related to persuasion. Humor, auditory memory devices, and brand-differentiating claims are the strongest executional factors related to this variate. By contrast, the first canonical variate to emerge for established product commercials is most strongly related to persuasion and is moderately related to recall and comprehension. Brand-differentiating claim is the dominant executional factor, and humor also has a strong relationship with this variate.

The three canonical variates for established products define a general performance variate led by persuasion, a recall variate slightly negative on persuasion, and a key message comprehension variate also slightly negative on persuasion. The first (persuasion) variate is related to brand-differentiating claims and humor. The second (recall) variate is related to storyboards/animatics, humor, time until product identification (negative), relevant setting, and brand prominence in the commercial. The third variate (comprehension) is related to product benefits, convenience of product usage, research findings (negative), time until product identification, and user satisfaction (negative). It is not surprising that the ability of the commercial to make a brand-differentiating claim is the dominant factor influencing persuasion. The influences on commercial-related recall are more diffuse—namely, use of animated characters, prominent product identification, humor, and commercial setting. Factors related to key message comprehension are typically those things that advertisers are most interested in getting across to the audience. Because the variates are orthogonal (that is, statistically independent of each other), the executional factors in each variate may be interpreted as more nearly pure measures of effectiveness.

Table 7–8
Canonical Variate Analysis for New Products

	Canonical Variate 1	Canonical Variate 2
Recall	.98	.19
Comprehension	.83	– .47
Persuasion	.46	– .54
Relevant setting (factor 1)	.064	– .117
Product benefits (factor 2)	– .019	.194
Time until identification (factor 3)	.010	.061
Product attributes/components (factor 4)	.073	.114
Cast (factor 5)	.121	.414
Stills/storyboard/animatics (factor 6)	.071	.294
Brand prominence (factor 7)	.281	– .178
Front-end impact (factor 8)	.188	– .113
User satisfaction (factor 9)	.086	– .139
Emotional tone (factor 10)	– .234	– .170
Humor (factor 11)	.543	.310
Auditory memory devices (factor 12)	.377	– .040
Company identification (factor 13)	– .013	– .444
Demonstration in use (factor 14)	.047	– .017
On-screen characters (factor 15)	.213	.315
Continuity (factor 16)	.132	– .121
Serious/graphics (factor 17)	.069	.143
Brand sign-off (factor 18)	.144	– .079
Indirect comparison (factor 19)	– .087	.037
Product reminder (factor 20)	.059	.194
Convenience in use (factor 21)	.273	– .139
Fantasy (factor 22)	.075	.125
Research (factor 23)	.041	– .143
Substantive supers (factor 24)	.121	– .066
Brand-differentiating claim	.419	– .277

For new products the variates are not as distinct. The first variate is a primary recall/comprehension variate that is moderately related to persuasion. Humor, auditory memory devices, and the presence of a brand-differentiating claim are most strongly associated with this variate. The second variate is related negatively to persuasion and comprehension. The executional factors with the strongest relationship to this variate are company identification (negative), number of on-screen characters, humor, animated

Table 7–9
Canonical Variate Analysis for Established Products

	Canonical Variate 1	Canonical Variate 2	Canonical Variate 3
Recall	.69	.57	.44
Comprehension	.58	−.11	.81
Persuasion	.87	−.36	−.33
Relevant setting (factor 1)	−.144	.268	.176
Product benefits (factor 2)	.060	.129	.512
Time until identification (factor 3)	−.011	−.348	.364
Product attributes/components (factor 4)	−.048	−.060	−.138
Cast (factor 5)	−.209	.201	−.153
Stills/storyboard/animatics (factor 6)	−.218	.436	−.102
Brand prominence (factor 7)	−.018	.286	−.038
Front-end impact (factor 8)	.008	−.003	.124
User satisfaction (factor 9)	−.240	.011	−.269
Emotional tone (factor 10)	.030	−.118	−.072
Humor (factor 11)	.359	.368	.160
Auditory memory devices (factor 12)	−.022	.224	.030
Company identification (factor 13)	007	−.240	.048
Demonstration in use (factor 14)	.012	−.222	−.111
On-screen characters (factor 15)	−.011	.152	.101
Continuity of action (factor 16)	.193	.066	−.087
Serious/graphics (factor 17)	.070	−.030	−.028
Brand sign-off (factor 18)	.087	.231	.050
Indirect comparison (factor 19)	.206	−.078	−.167
Product reminder (factor 20)	−.169	.239	−.060
Convenience in use (factor 21)	−.259	−.025	.402
Fantasy (factor 22)	.081	.177	−.233
Research (factor 23)	.124	.025	−.388
Substantive supers (factor 24)	.227	−.094	−.144
Brand-differentiating claim	.780	.022	−.144

characters/storyboard, and brand-differentiating claims (negative). This variate might well be regarded as an attention/distraction factor, one in which the executional elements compete with the key message for audience attention. It is worthy of note that the persuasion measure was not particularly prominent in either of the variates for new product commercials, while it was the dominant performance measure in one of the variates for the established products. This is consistent with the regression findings in which only half as much variance in new product persuasion is accounted for by executional factors compared to established product persuasion.

These results suggest a fundamental difference in the nature of the relationships between persuasion and executional factors for new and established products. For established products, the executional factors influencing persuasion are more distinct from the factors affecting recall and comprehension. For new products, the factors affecting persuasion, comprehension, and recall appear to be less separable. The process resulting from new product commercial exposure appears to be largely recall driven, while the processes for established products and the executional factors causing them are much more varied and rich.

Established products have been visible to consumers for some time. There have been multiple opportunities for consumers to hear of the product. Recall of any one commercial execution is less important to consumer choice than for a new product, where exposure to the product is limited to the commercial. Attitude formation for new products is heavily dependent first on commercial recall. The persuasiveness of a commercial for an established product would not depend on recall of a specific execution. Factors related to commercial performance may be mediated by preexisting levels of commercial recall and general awareness of the product. An analysis designed to investigate the mediating impact of recall on commercial performance is reported in the next section.

Impact of Level of Recall on the Relationship of Advertising Execution and Advertising Effectiveness

The average related recall for all 1,059 commercials in the dataset was 30 percent. This average level appeared to be a reasonable breakpoint for classifying commercials as high- or low-recall commercials. Separate analyses were carried out on each set. Table 7–10 reports the simple Pearson product moment correlation coefficients between executional factors and performance measures for each commercial set. For commercials attaining above-average recall, brand-differentiating message is a significant factor. For commercials with below-average recall, there is no relationship between brand-differentiating message and recall, and brand-differentiating message is negatively associated with comprehension. The relationship between persuasion and brand-differentiating message, while positive, is only a third of the strength of the relationship when recall is above average. Recall appears to moderate significantly the relationship between brand-differentiating message and all three measures of commercial effectiveness.

Other differences noted include the following:

1. Emphasis on product attributes and ingredients has a more negative impact on persuasion when recall is above average.

2. The presence of a cast of on-screen characters has a more negative impact on key message comprehension when recall is above average.

3. Information on user satisfaction has a positive relationship when recall is below average and a negative relationship when recall is above average.

4. Company identification has a negative influence on recall and comprehension when recall is below average but a positive influence when recall is above average.

5. Product reminder has a negative relationship with commercial performance, but its negative effect is accentuated when recall is above average.

6. Research information has a complex relationship with recall: positive effect on recall and negative effect on persuasion for below-average recall commercials. When recall is above average, research information has an apparent positive effect on persuasion.

Regression analyses designed to identify predictors of each of the three measures of effectiveness were carried out for the high- and low-recall commercials. These analyses are reported in tables 7–11 through 7–16. In the analyses of both comprehension and persuasion, the executional factors account for twice as much variation among the above-average recall commercials than among the below-average recall commercials. High recall appears to heighten the effects of executional variables.

The factors related to recall for high-recall commercials are different from the relationships for the low-recall group, with the single exception of demonstration of the product in use (tables 7–11 and 7–12). The reason for these differences may be that the executional devices appearing in the high-recall commercials are decidedly less likely to occur in the low-recall commercials. Humor is much more likely to occur in high-recall commercials. By the same token, it is not the case that graphics work in low-recall commercials but not in high-recall commercials; rather, most commercials with graphics tend to be concentrated among low-recall commercials. The results for recall may be due more to restrictions of range and numbers of observations than to differences in fundamental processes. This same restriction of range problem may also explain some of the differences observed for the comprehension measure.

Differences in the results observed for persuasion are less likely to be due to restricted range since persuasion is not highly correlated with recall (tables

Table 7-10
Pearson Product Moment Correlations between Executional Factors and Measures of Effectiveness for Commercials Attaining Below-and Above-Average Recall

	Recall		Comprehension		Persuasion	
	Below	*Above*	*Below*	*Above*	*Below*	*Above*
Relevant setting (factor 1)	.06	.01	.09	.05	-.03	-.02
Product benefits (factor 2)	.08	.04	.14	.14	-.01	.07
Time until identification (factor 3)	-.11	.00	.01	.06	.01	-.05
Product attributes/ingredients (factor 4)	-.12	-.06	-.07	-.09	-.01	-.11
Cast (factor 5)	.07	.04	-.01	-.19	-.13	-.17
Storyboard/animatics (factor 6)	.10	.04	-.10	-.11	-.03	-.09
Brand prominence (factor 7)	-.04	.04	-.01	.01	-.00	.02
Front-end impact (factor 8)	.06	.08	.04	.09	.03	.07
User satisfaction (factor 9)	.12	-.12	.08	-.08	.04	-.06
Emotional tone (factor 10)	-.05	-.07	-.05	-.09	.03	-.01
Humor (factor 11)	.14	.20	.03	.03	.05	-.02
Auditory memory devices (factor 12)	.14	.14	.04	.06	.03	-.01
Company identification (factor 13)	-.05	.07	-.04	.22	.05	.09
Demonstration in use (factor 14)	.18	-.07	.02	.00	.05	.01
On-screen characters (factor 15)	.06	-.07	-.03	-.07	-.04	-.08

Continuity (factor 16)	−.03	.08	−.04	.03	.07	.09
Serious/graphics (factor 17)	.01	−.03	.00	.02	−.04	−.02
Brand sign-off (factor 18)	.02	.07	−.03	.05	−.01	.00
Indirect comparison (factor 19)	.03	−.02	.04	−.05	.02	.04
Product reminder (factor 20)	−.03	−.11	−.04	−.16	−.04	−.13
Convenience in use (factor 21)	−.01	.08	.12	.13	.03	.02
Fantasy (factor 22)	.06	.01	−.03	−.02	−.07	.00
Research (factor 23)	.11	−.03	.01	−.05	−.07	.09
Substantive supers (factor 24)	.02	.01	.01	.01	.08	−.01
Brand-differentiating message	−.03	.19	−.14	.24	.11	.33

Table 7-11
Prediction of Recall for Commercials Scoring above Average on Recall (Recall Greater than 30 Percent)

	Multiple R	Beta[a]
Humor (factor 11)	.20	.18
Brand-differentiating message	.26	.17
Demonstration in use (factor 14)	.28	−.12
Time until identification (factor 3)	.31	.11
Auditory memory device (factor 12)	.32	.10

Multiple R = .32
R^2 = .10
Adjusted R^2 = .09
[a]Standardized regression coefficients, all significant at the .05 level.

Table 7-12
Prediction of Recall for Commercials Scoring below Average on Recall (Recall Less than 30 Percent)

	Multiple R	Beta[a]
Serious/graphics (factor 17)	.23	.23
Product benefits (factor 2)	.30	.20
Convenience in use (factor 35)	.35	−.17
Company identification (factor 13)	.37	−.10
Research (factor 23)	.38	.11
Substantive supers (factor 24)	.39	.09
Demonstration in use (factor 14)	.40	−.08
Product reminder (factor 20)	.41	.08

Multiple R = .41
R^2 = .17
Adjusted R^2 = .15
[a]Standardized regression coefficients, all significant at the .05 level.

7-15 and 7-16). Brand-differentiating message and convenience of use are significant positive predictors of persuasion for both high- and low-recall commercials. In the case of high-recall commercials, these two items account for 12 percent of the variance, while they account for only 2 percent of the variance among low-recall commercials. Recall, while not usually highly correlated with persuasion, has a strong moderating effect on the relationships between persuasion and executional factors.

Table 7–13
Prediction of Comprehension for Commercials, Scoring above Average on Recall (Recall Greater than 30 Percent)

	Multiple R	*Beta*[a]
Brand-differentiating message	.22	.21
Company identification (factor 13)	.26	.12
Cast (factor 5)	.29	− .12
Time until identification (factor 3)	.32	.13
Product reminder (factor 20)	.34	− .12
Front-end impact (factor 8)	.35	.10
Convenience in use (factor 21)	.37	.09

Multiple R = .37
R^2 = .13
Adjusted R^2 = .12
[a]Standardized regression coefficients, all significant at the .05 level.

Table 7–14
Prediction of Comprehension for Commercials Scoring below Average on Recall (Recall Less than 30 Percent)

	Multiple R	*Beta*[a]
Serious graphics (factor 17)	.16	.21
Storyboard/animatics (factor 6)	.22	.25
Demonstration in use (factor 14)	.24	.23
Time until identification (factor 3)	.25	.22
Product benefits (factor 2)	.27	.22

Multiple R = .27
R^2 = .07
Adjusted R^2 = .06
[a]Standardized regression coefficients, all significant at the .05 level.

Table 7–15
Prediction of Persuasion for Commercials Scoring above Average on Recall (Recall Greater than 30 Percent)

	Multiple R	*Beta*[a]
Brand-differentiating message	.33	.29
Product reminder (factor 20)	.37	− .16
Continuity (factor 16)	.40	.12
Convenience in use (factor 21)	.41	.09

Multiple R = .41
R^2 = .17
Adjusted R^2 = .15
[a]Standardized regression coefficients, all significant at the .05 level.

Table 7–16
Prediction of Persuasion for Commercials Scoring below
Average on Recall (Recall Less than 30 Percent)

	Multiple R	*Beta*[a]
Brand-differentiating message	.11	.23
Storyboard/animatics (factor 6)	.15	.24
Substantive supers (factor 24)	.18	.24
Convenience in use (factor 21)	.20	.24
Company identification (factor 13)	.22	.22

Multiple R = .22
R^2 = .05
Adjusted R^2 = .04
[a]Standardized regression coefficients, all significant at the .05 level.

Impact of Persuasion on the Relationship of Advertising Execution and Advertising Effectiveness

It is conceivable that relationships between executional factors and measures of advertising performance are different for those commercials that exceed expected switching rates compared to those commercials that do not. A series of analyses were carried out to investigate this hypothesis. Commercials were divided into two groups based on whether they scored above or below their expected persuasion score (Fair Share). Table 7–17 shows the Pearson product moment correlations between executional factors and the measures of advertising performance for these two sets of commercials. When commercials are above average on the persuasion measure, then brand prominence, front-end impact, company identification, demonstration of the product in use, continuity, convenience, and brand-differentiating claims appear to work better.

Regression analyses predicting related recall for above and below Fair Share persuasion commercials produced rather different results (tables 7–18 and 7–19). Humor was the only executional factor to emerge in both high- and low-persuasion equations. Brand-differentiating message is the strongest predictor of recall for high-persuasion commercials and does not even appear as a significant predictor of recall for low-persuasion commercials. Executional factors account for 12 percent of the variance in comprehension for high-persuasion commercials but only 2 percent for commercials below Fair Share (tables 7–20 and 7–21). Brand-differentiating message and convenience in use are the two best predictors of comprehension for high-persuasion commercials, together accounting for over 9 percent of the total variation.

Prediction of persuasion among high- and low-persuasion commercials is particularly interesting. Convenience in use and brand-differentiating message are significant predictors in both sets of commercials (tables 7–22 and 7–23); convenience in use is positive for high-persuasion commercials and negative for low-persuasion commercials. For high-persuasion commercials, persuasion appears to be primarily a function of reasons for purchasing the product (convenience, brand-differentiating message, and company identification) and communication effectiveness (continuity and brand prominence). Factors predicting persuasion among low-persuasion commercials are a hodge-podge of items, some related to message, some to format, and some to the presence of supporting evidence (research).

It is useful to compare table 7–15 with table 7–22. Three items that predict persuasion for high-recall commercials also emerge in the analysis of persuasion among high-persuasion commercials: brand-differentiating message, continuity, and convenience of the product in use. The same basic factors that predict persuasion among high-recall commercials also predict persuasion among high-persuasion commercials. This is not the case for low-recall and low-persuasion commercials. There appear to be many ways to fail, but few ways to succeed.

It is worth noting that expected persuasion (Fair Share) is a poor predictor of both recall and comprehension. Fair Share accounts for 2 percent of the variance of related recall and less than 1 percent of the variance of the comprehension measure.

Grouping Commercials by Performance on Measures of Advertising Effectiveness

Another way to examine the relationships between commercial execution and measures of performance is to profile commercials based on their performance across all three measures. Table 7–24 provides a summary of the characteristics of eight different performance profiles. These commercials have been grouped based on combinations of above- or below-average scores on the three performance measures.

Given these eight commercial profiles, discriminant analyses were carried out to determine the degree to which executional factors differentiate among the groups. Two statistically significant discriminant functions were found to account for approximately 21 percent of the variation among the groups. Table 7–25 provides the correlations between individual executional factors and each discriminant function and the mean scores of the eight groups on each discriminant function. The results of the analysis are consistent with findings reported previously.

The first discriminant function is positively related to brand-differentiating message and convenience in use and negatively related to background cast and product attributes/ingredients. The second function is positively related to humor, animated principal character, number of on-screen characters,

Table 7-17
Pearson Product Moment Correlations between Executional Factors and Measures of Advertising Effectiveness for Commercials Scoring below and above Fair Share Persuasion

	Recall		Comprehension		Persuasion	
	Below	*Above*	*Below*	*Above*	*Below*	*Above*
Relevant setting (factor 1)	.07	.10	.10	.09	−.05	.06
Product benefits (factor 2)	.01	.03	.11	.08	−.05	.02
Time until identification (factor 3)	−.06	−.09	.04	−.01	.06	−.07
Product attributes/ingredients (factor 4)	−.12	−.14	−.11	−.13	.01	−.17
Cast (factor 5)	.03	.01	−.05	−.12	−.03	−.13
Storyboard/animatics (factor 6)	.20	.01	−.02	−.02	−.04	.06
Brand prominence (factor 7)	.08	.09	.03	.09	−.04	.13
Front-end impact (factor 8)	.05	.09	.06	.08	−.01	.07
User satisfaction (factor 9)	−.03	−.09	−.02	−.07	.05	−.03
Emotional tone (factor 10)	−.01	−.09	−.01	−.11	.07	.00
Humor (factor 11)	.23	.25	.10	.12	.09	−.02

Auditory memory devices (factor 12)	.14	.13	.07	.09	.01	.00
Company identification (factor 13)	-.12	.07	-.03	.17	-.03	.09
Demonstration in use (factor 14)	.11	-.03	.06	-.02	-.06	.05
On-screen characters (factor 15)	.10	.02	.01	.00	-.02	-.04
Continuity (factor 16)	.03	.11	-.03	.10	.07	.07
Serious/graphics (factor 17)	-.08	-.05	-.00	-.05	-.01	-.03
Brand sign-off (factor 18)	.08	.06	.01	.07	-.05	.00
Indirect comparison (factor 19)	.03	.00	.00	-.02	.03	-.01
Product reminder (factor 20)	.05	-.11	-.06	-.09	-.07	-.04
Convenience in use (factor 21)	.04	.15	.09	.11	-.12	.08
Fantasy (factor 22)	.03	.04	-.03	.01	-.04	-.03
Research (factor 23)	-.04	-.05	-.08	-.06	.04	.03
Substantive supers (factor 24)	-.02	-.01	-.03	-.00	.02	-.11
Brand-differentiating message	-.01	.25	-.09	.29	.13	.21

Table 7–18
Prediction of Recall for Commercials Scoring above Expected Persuasion (Persuasion Greater than Fair Share)

	Multiple R	Beta[a]
Brand-differentiating message	.24	.25
Humor (factor 11)	.34	.24
Demonstration in use (factor 14)	.36	−.13
Convenience in use (factor 21)	.38	.13
Front-end impact (factor 8)	.40	.11
Brand prominence (factor 7)	.41	.10

Multiple R = .41
R^2 = .17
Adjusted R^2 = .16
[a]Standardized regression coefficients, all significant at the .05 level.

Table 7–19
Prediction of Recall for Commercials Scoring below Expected Persuasion (Fair Share Greater than Persuasion)

	Multiple R	Beta[a]
Humor (factor 11)	.20	.20
Company identification (factor 13)	.25	−.15
Storyboard (factor 6)	.28	.13
On-screen character (factor 15)	.31	.12
Auditory memory devices (factor 12)	.32	.09
Product reminder (factor 26)	.33	.08
Product benefits (factor 34)	.34	.08

Multiple R = .34
R^2 = .12
Adjusted R^2 = .11
[a]Standardized regression coefficients, all significant at the .05 level.

product reminder, and brand prominence. Company identification and serious tone/graphics are negatively related to this function. The first function may be thought of as a reasons-to-buy function (brand differentiation), while the second function appears to be related more to the ability of the commercial to gain attention and stimulate memory. It is not surprising that commercial profile A, scoring above average on all three measures of effectiveness, has the highest means on both of these functions. Excluding profiles

Table 7–20
**Prediction of Comprehension for Commercials Scoring above
Expected Persuasion (Persuasion Greater than Fair Share)**

	Multiple R	*Beta*[a]
Brand-differentiating message	.27	.30
Convenience in use (factor 21)	.32	.18
Front-end impact (factor 8)	.34	.11
Humor (factor 11)	.36	.11

Multiple R = .36
R^2 = .13
Adjusted R^2 = .12
[a]Standardized regression coefficients, all significant at the .05 level.

Table 7–21
**Prediction of Comprehension for Commercials Scoring below
Expected Persuasion (Fair Share Greater than Persuasion)**

	Multiple R	*Beta*[a]
Humor (factor 11)	.11	.11
Time until identification (factor 3)	.14	.09

Multiple R = .14
R^2 = .02
Adjusted R^2 = .02
[a]Standardized regression coefficients, all significant at the .05 level.

Table 7–22
**Prediction of Persuasion for Commercials Scoring above
Expected Persuasion (Persuasion Greater than Fair Share)**

	Multiple R	*Beta*[a]
Brand prominence (factor 7)	.17	.16
Convenience in use (factor 21)	.24	.17
Brand-differentiating message	.28	.13
Company identification (factor 13)	.30	.11
Continuity (factor 16)	.32	.10

Multiple R = .32
R^2 = .10
Adjusted R^2 = .09
[a]Standardized regression coefficients, all significant at the .05 level.

Table 7–23
Prediction of Persuasion for Commercials Scoring below
Expected Persuasion (Fair Share Greater than Persuasion)

	Multiple R	Beta[a]
Brand-differentiating message	.18	.12
Storyboard/animatics (factor 6)	.25	−.16
Time until identification (factor 3)	.28	.13
Relevant setting (factor 1)	.30	−.14
Research (factor 23)	.32	.11
Convenience in use (factor 21)	.33	−.12
Auditory memory devices (factor 12)	.35	−.11
Product attributes/ingredients (factor 4)	.36	.10

Multiple R = .36
R^2 = .13
Adjusted R^2 = .12
[a]Standardized regression coefficients, all significant at the .05 level.

C, E, and F, which are problematic because of their small sample size and confounding with particular types of commercials, the major profiles are interpretable. It is interesting that commercials in profile H (below average on all three performance measures) would be the most difficult to classify with these functions. Again, there appear to be few ways to succeed but many ways to fail.

While these results are consistent with previous analyses, they also point out the exceptions to the general relationships identified. Some commercials score well on persuasion without high levels of recall or comprehension. Above-average levels of key message comprehension may be achieved even when recall is below average.

Effects of Prechoice on Advertising Execution and
Measures of Effectiveness

One factor that may influence the impact of executional devices on advertising performance is current market share of users. In the present study, a reasonable surrogate for share of users is prechoice, the number of respondents selecting a particular brand prior to exposure to the test commercial, although prechoice tends to be skewed upward from actual share of users. For established products the average prechoice is 18.5 percent. Three hundred forty-five commercials are for established products with less

Table 7-24
Commercials Grouped by Level of Performance on the Three Measures of Effectiveness

	Percent Average Recall	Percent Average Comprehension	Percent Average Adjusted Persuasion	Percent Average Prechoice	Percent New or Improved Products	Average Switching	Average Number of Brands
A. Commercials above average on recall, comprehension and persuasion (N = 148)	47	32	5.0	11	55	33.16	7.42
B. Commercials above average on recall and comprehension but below average on persuasion (N = 143)	40	23	-2.0	18	29	23.34	9.41
C. Commercials above average on recall, below average on comprehension, and above average on persuasion (N = 47)	36	9	3.0	8	66	30.58	7.90
D. Commercials above average on recall but below average on comprehension and persuasion (N = 111)	37	8	-2.0	18	43	23.91	9.72
E. Commercials below average on recall but above average on comprehension and persuasion (N = 34)	26	18	2.0	6	65	31.28	7.98
F. Commercials below average on recall, above average on comprehension, and below average on persuasion (N = 42)	24	17	-2.0	11	36	25.94	10.10
G. Commercials below average on both recall and comprehension but above average on persuasion (N = 112)	21	8	1.5	2	74	30.26	8.03
H. Commercials below average on recall, comprehension, and persuasion (N = 358)	20	7	-2.0	9	41	25.16	11.62

Table 7–25
Executional Factors Differentiating Commercials, by Level of Performance on the Three Measures of Effectiveness

	Discriminant Function 1: Brand Differentiation	*Discriminant Function 2: Attention*
Discriminant loadings		
Brand-differentiating message	.54	
Product attributes/ingredients (factor 4)	– .31	
Cast (factor 5)	– .30	
Convenience in use (factor 20)	.28	
Humor (factor 11)		.45
Storyboard/animatics (factor 6)		.36
On-screen characters (factor 15)		.34
Product reminder (factor 20)		.33
Company identification (factor 13)		– .33
Brand prominence (factor 7)		.31
Serious graphics (factor 17)		– .20
Mean scores of commercials on discriminant functions		
A. Above average on recall, comprehension, and persuasion	.72	.44
B. Above average on recall and comprehension, below average on persuasion	– .17	.12
C. Above average on recall and persuasion, below average on comprehension	.46	– .14
D. Above average on recall, below average on comprehension and persuasion	– .13	.18
E. Below average on recall, above average on comprehension and persuasion	– .38	.07
F. Below average on recall, above average on comprehension, and below average on persuasion	– .39	.27
G. Below average on recall and comprehension, above average on persuasion	.21	.01
H. Below average on recall, comprehension, and persuasion	.22	.30
Overall mean	.00	.00

than 18.5 percent prechoice, and 175 commercials are for established products with greater than 18.5 percent prechoice. Regression analyses designed to examine the relationships between executional factors and measures of effectiveness were carried out separately for commercials with above-average and below-average prechoice.

Two factors are common to the prediction of recall for high-share and low-share brands: brand-differentiating claim and company identification. Brand-differentiating claim is positively related to recall in both analyses but is decidedly stronger for high-share brands (tables 7–26 and 7–27). Company identification is negatively related to recall in both analyses. For high-share brands, brand sign-off is the only factor other than brand-differentiating message with a positive relationship. For low-share brands, humor has the strongest positive relationship, followed by brand-differentiating message, product benefits, and brand prominence.

Table 7–26
Prediction of Recall for Established Products with Above-Average Prechoice shares (Prechoice Greater than 18.5)
(N = 179)

	Multiple R	*Beta*[a]
Brand-differentiating message	.37	.35
User satisfaction (factor 9)	.40	−.16
Brand sign-off (factor 18)	.43	.18
Company identification (factor 13)	.45	−.14
Demonstration in use (factor 14)	.47	−.14

Multiple R = .47
R^2 = .22
Adjusted R^2 = .20
[a]Standardized regression coefficients, all significant at the .05 level.

Table 7–27
Prediction of Recall for Established Products with Below-Average Prechoice Shares (Prechoice Less than 18.5)
(N = 345)

	Multiple R	*Beta*[a]
Humor (factor 11)	.29	.17
Brand-differentiating message	.34	.18
Product benefits (factor 2)	.36	.14
Brand prominence (factor 7)	.38	.14
Company identification (factor 13)	.40	−.11
On-screen characters (factor 15)	.41	.11

Multiple R = .41
R^2 = .17
Adjusted R^2 = .16
[a]Standardized regression coefficients, all significant at the .05 level.

Executional factors account for decidedly more variance in the comprehension measure for high-share brands than for low-share brands (tables 7–28 and 7–29). For high-share brands, brand-differentiating message is again the strongest predictor of comprehension. It is not as strong a predictor for low-share brands.

Despite the differences observed in the analyses for recall and comprehension, the results of the analyses for persuasion are quite similar for both high- and low-share brand commercials, but twice as much variance is accounted for by executional factors in the high-share brand analysis. All four significant predictors of low-share brand persuasion appear in the high-share

Table 7–28
Prediction of Comprehension for Established Products with Above-Average Prechoice Shares (Prechoice Greater than 18.5) *(N = 179)*

	Multiple R	*Beta*[a]
Brand-differentiating message	.26	.26
User satisfaction (factor 9)	.32	−.16
Product attributes/components (factor 4)	.36	−.18
Brand prominence (factor 7)	.40	−.20
Research (factor 23)	.43	−.16
Convenience in use (factor 21)	.45	.14

Multiple R = .45
R^2 = .20
Adjusted R^2 = .18
[a]Standardized regression coefficients, all significant at the .05 level.

Table 7–29
Prediction of Comprehension for Established Products with Below-Average Prechoice Shares (Prechoice Less than 18.5) *(N = 345)*

	Multiple R	*Beta*[a]
Humor (factor 11)	.20	.19
Time until identification (factor 3)	.23	.13
Brand-differentiating message	.27	.13

Multiple R = .27
R^2 = .07
Adjusted R^2 = .06
[a]Standardized regression coefficients, all significant at the .05 level.

brand analysis, and the directions of the relationships are the same (tables 7–30 and 7–31). The additional factors influencing high-share brands are indirect comparisons and relevant product setting.

Product Category, Manufacturer, Subcategory, and Brand Effects

Some previous research has identified differences in the relationships of advertising execution and measures of advertising effectiveness related to

Table 7–30
Prediction of Persuasion for Established Products with Above-Average Prechoice Shares (Prechoice Greater than 18.5) *(N = 179)*

	Multiple R	Beta[a]
Brand-differentiating message	.34	.28
Relevant setting (factor 1)	.42	− .22
User satisfaction (factor 9)	.47	− .18
Indirect comparison (factor 19)	.50	.20
Storyboard (factor 6)	.52	− .14
Product reminder (factor 20)	.53	− .13

Multiple R = .53
R^2 = .29
Adjusted R^2 = .26
[a]Standardized regression coefficients, all significant at the .05 level.

Table 7–31
Prediction of Persuasion for Established Products with Below-Average Prechoice Shares (Prechoice Less than 18.5) *(N = 345)*

	Multiple R	Beta[a]
Brand-differentiating message	.25	.25
Storyboard (factor 6)	.35	− .25
User satisfaction (factor 9)	.37	− .12
Product reminder (factor 20)	.38	− .11

Multiple R = .38
R^2 = .14
Adjusted R^2 = .13
[a]Standardized regression coefficients, all significant at the .05 level.

product category and brand differences. The present study examined such differences and sought to determine the extent to which the presence of commercials for a particular manufacturer, subcategory, or brand influenced the results. Regression analyses designed to predict related recall, key message comprehension, and persuasion were carried out within each of the twelve general product categories identified earlier. Although differences emerged, closer examination revealed that they were driven primarily by restrictions of range on both the executional factors and measures of advertising effectiveness. For example, product attributes/ingredients emerges as a significant negative predictor of persuasion for small durables, snack foods, and entrees and side dishes, but there are other categories where product attributes/ingredients would be appropriate information, but it does not appear with great enough frequency to emerge as a significant predictor. This finding has some important implications for future research. Before concluding that product category by executional factor interactions exist, and they probably do, the frequency and variance of executional factors should be carefully examined.

Since differences in frequency and range of executional factors do exist across product categories, it is important to examine the robustness of the results obtained. Findings that result from the presence of a particular product category, manufacturer, or brand in the dataset suggest a lack of generality of the findings to the larger dataset. To investigate the robustness of the results reported here, a series of analyses were run in which each product category, one at a time, was dropped from the dataset and the analyses were rerun. This series of analyses produced results virtually identical to those for the total dataset.

The same series of analyses was run for manufacturers, product subcategories, and brands. Each of the seven manufacturers with 5 percent or more of the commercials in the total database was eliminated in turn, and the analyses were rerun. The five most frequent subcategories were dropped in turn, as were brands representing at least 1 percent of the total database. The results of each of these analyses were nearly identical to those obtained with the full database. These analyses suggest that the general results are not a function of a single product category, subcategory, manufacturer, or brand.

Analysis of Commercials with High and Low Switching Rates

The measurement of brand switching within a category was discussed in chapter 4. A wide range of switching rates was present in the dataset. Average switching within a product subcategory ranged from 7 to 62 percent, with a mean of 27 percent. The median switching rate was 26 percent, and the modal switching value was 27 percent. To investigate the moderating effects of rate of switching on the relationship between executional factors and measures of advertising effectiveness, the dataset was split into a high-switching group (greater than 27 percent) and a low-switching group (less than 27 percent). Four hundred six commercials were for products in the high-switching group, and 651 were for products in the low-switching group.

Twice as much of the variance in the recall measure was accounted for by advertising execution in the high-switching group as in the low-switching group. The results of these regression analyses are presented in tables 7–32 and 7–33. Brand-differentiating message is the single most important executional factor related to recall among high-switching products, accounting for over 9 percent of the total variance. While a brand-differentiating message is also a significant predictor of recall in the low-switching group, it accounts for decidedly less variance. More important in the low-switching group are humor, product benefits, and brand prominence.

The results of the analysis for key message comprehension, shown in tables 7–34 and 7–35, are similar to those for recall. Twice as much of the total variation in comprehension is accounted for by executional factors in the high-switching group as in the low-switching group. Brand-differentiating claim is the single most important predictor of comprehension in the high-switching group. It is significant, but far less important, in the low-switching group of commercials.

Results of the analyses for persuasion indicate that brand-differentiating claim is the most important executional factor affecting both low- and high-switching groups (tables 7–36 and 7–37). Slightly more variance is accounted for in the high- than in the low-switching group.

Table 7–32
Prediction of Recall for Commercials for Products in High-Switching Categories
(N = 406)

	Multiple R	*Beta*[a]
Brand-differentiating message	.32	.31
Humor (factor 11)	.42	.29
Auditory memory devices (factor 12)	.44	.13
Front-end impact (factor 8)	.45	.11
Brand sign-off (factor 18)	.46	.11

Multiple R = .46
R^2 = .21
Adjusted R^2 = .20
[a]Standardized regression coefficients, all significant at the .05 level.

Table 7–33
Prediction of Recall for Commercials for Products in Low-Switching Categories
(N = 651)

	Multiple R	*Beta*[a]
Humor (factor 11)	.17	.17
Product benefits (factor 2)	.21	.12
Brand prominence (factor 7)	.24	.09
Auditory memory device (factor 12)	.26	.11
On-screen characters (factor 15)	.27	.09
Company identification (factor 13)	.28	−.09
Brand-differentiating message	.30	.11
Product attributes/ingredients (factor 4)	.31	−.09
Storyboard/animatics (factor 6)	.32	.08

Multiple R = .32
R^2 = .10
Adjusted R^2 = .09
[a]Standardized regression coefficients, all significant at the .05 level.

Table 7–34
Prediction of Comprehension for Commercials for Products in High-Switching Categories
(N = 406)

	Multiple R	*Beta*[a]
Brand-differentiating message	.30	.27
Humor (factor 11)	.34	.19
Cast (factor 5)	.36	−.13
Front-end impact (factor 8)	.38	.11
Brand sign-off (factor 18)	.39	.11
Convenience in use (factor 21)	.40	.09

Multiple R = .40
R^2 = .16
Adjusted R^2 = .15
[a]Standardized regression coefficients, all significant at the .05 level.

Table 7–35
Prediction of Comprehension for Commercials for Products in Low-Switching Categories
(N = 651)

	Multiple R	*Beta*[a]
Convenience in use (factor 21)	.12	.14
Product reminder (factor 20)	.16	−.10
Time until identification (factor 3)	.18	.09
Auditory memory devices (factor 12)	.20	.09
Brand-differentiating message	.21	.09
Product benefits (factor 2)	.22	.08

Multiple R = .22
R^2 = .05
Adjusted R^2 = .04
[a]Standardized regression coefficients, all significant at the .05 level.

Table 7–36
Prediction of Persuasion for Commercials for Products in High-Switching Categories
(N = 406)

	Multiple R	*Beta*[a]
Brand-differentiating message	.30	.26
Cast (factor 3)	.34	−.17
Front-end impact (factor 8)	.36	.12
Continuity (factor 16)	.38	.10

Multiple R = .38
R^2 = .14
Adjusted R^2 = .13
[a]Standardized regression coefficients, all significant at the .05 level.

Analysis of Relationships of Executional Factors and Measures of Advertising Effectiveness by Number of Brands

Products in a category may include regional, local, store, and national brands, depending on how a Research Systems Corporation client chooses to define the competitive set. Since the number of brands may vary from city to

Table 7–37
Prediction of Persuasion for Commercials for Products in Low-Switching Categories
(N = 652)

	Multiple R	Beta[a]
Brand-differentiating message	.20	.17
Time until identification (factor 3)	.23	.12
Product benefits (factor 2)	.25	−.12
Storyboard/animatics (factor 6)	.27	−.10
Convenience in use (factor 21)	.28	−.09
Relevant setting (factor 1)	.29	−.08

Multiple R = .29
R^2 = .09
Adjusted R^2 = .08
[a]Standardized regression coefficients, all significant at the .05 level.

city, and Research Systems Corporation may test a commercial in four different cities, the average number of brands may not be a whole number. In the present dataset, the number of brands in a category ranged from 2.8 to 30, with a mean of 9.7. The median was 9 and the modal value was 8. To examine the influence of number of brands on the relationships between executional factors and measures of advertising effectiveness, the commercials in the dataset were divided into commercials for products in categories of ten or more brands, and commercials for products in categories with fewer than ten brands. Separate regression analyses were carried out for each of these groups. These analyses are reported in tables 7–38 to 7–43.

Table 7–38
Prediction of Recall for Commercials for Product Categories with Ten or More Brands
(N = 475)

	Multiple R	Beta[a]
Humor (factor 11)	.35	.34
Brand-differentiating message	.38	.17
Auditory memory devices (factor 12)	.42	.15
On-screen characters (factor 15)	.43	.13
Emotional tone (factor 10)	.45	−.11
Product benefits (factor 2)	.45	.09

Multiple R = .45
R^2 = .21
Adjusted R^2 = .20
[a]Standardized regression coefficients, all significant at the .05 level.

Table 7–39
Prediction of Recall for Commercials for Product Categories with Fewer than Ten Brands
(N = 584)

	Multiple R	*Beta*[a]
Brand-differentiating message	.20	.19
Company identification (factor 13)	.23	−.13
Humor (factor 11)	.26	.13
Brand prominence (factor 7)	.29	.12
User satisfaction (factor 9)	.30	−.09
Auditory memory device (factor 12)	.31	.09

Multiple R = .31
R^2 = .10
Adjusted R^2 = .09
[a]Standardized regression coefficients, all significant at the .05 level.

Table 7–40
Prediction of Comprehension for Commercials for Product Categories with Ten or More Brands
(N = 475)

	Multiple R	*Beta*[a]
Humor (factor 11)	.22	.23
Cast (factor 5)	.25	−.11
Convenience in use (factor 21)	.26	.10
Company identification (factor 13)	.28	.10

Multiple R = .28
R^2 = .08
Adjusted R^2 = .07
[a]Standardized regression coefficients, all significant at the .05 level.

Table 7–41
Prediction of Comprehension for Commercials for Product Categories with Fewer than Ten Brands
(N = 584)

	Multiple R	*Beta*[a]
Brand-differentiating message	.22	.24
User satisfaction (factor 9)	.25	−.11
Auditory memory devices (factor 12)	.27	.11
Convenience in use (factor 21)	.29	.10
Front-end impact (factor 8)	.30	.08

Multiple R = .30
R^2 = .09
Adjusted R^2 = .08
[a]Standardized regression coefficients, all significant at the .05 level.

Table 7–42
Prediction of Persuasion for Commercials for Product Categories with Ten or More Brands
(N = 475)

	Multiple R	Beta[a]
Brand-differentiating message	.15	.15
Cast (factor 5)	.19	−.12
Product reminder (factor 20)	.23	−.13
Auditory memory devices (factor 12)	.25	.10
Research (factor 23)	.27	.09
Storyboard/animatics (factor 6)	.28	−.09
Brand prominence (factor 7)	.30	−.09

Multiple R = .30
R^2 = .09
Adjusted R^2 = .07
[a]Standardized regression coefficients, all significant at the .05 level.

Table 7–43
Prediction of Persuasion for Commercials for Product Categories with Fewer than Ten Brands
(N = 584)

	Multiple R	Beta[a]
Brand-differentiating message	.31	.28
Front-end impact (factor 8)	.32	.10
Brand prominence (factor 7)	.33	.09
Continuity (factor 16)	.34	.08
Cast (factor 5)	.35	−.08

Multiple R = .35
R^2 = .12
Adjusted R^2 = .12
[a]Standardized regression coefficients, all significant at the .05 level.

The results suggest that advertising execution has a stronger impact on recall among commercials for products competing against a larger number of competitors. The amount of variation in persuasion attributable to execution is greater for brands with fewer competitors in the category, and the presence of a brand-differentiating claim is a much stronger predictor of persuasion among commercials for products with fewer competitors.

Live versus Storyboard/ Animatic Commercials

Seven hundred sixty-four of the commercials in the database were live commercials, while 293 were either storyboard or animatics. An analysis of the live commercials produced results almost identical to those obtained for the total dataset. Results of the storyboard/animatic commericals are reported in tables 7–44 to 7–46. These results are also similar to those for the total database, except that brand-differentiating claim emerges as a significant predictor of persuasion only. Recall is driven primarily by attention and mem-

. **Table 7–44**
Prediction of Recall for Animatic and Storyboard Commercials
(N = 293)

	Multiple R	Beta[a]
Humor (factor 11)	.23	.19
Front-end impact (factor 8)	.31	.18
Substantive supers (factor 24)	.34	.13
Brand prominence (factor 7)	.36	.14
On-screen characters (factor 15)	.39	.13

Multiple R = .39
R^2 = .15
Adjusted R^2 = .13
[a]Standardized regression coefficients, all significant at the .05 level.

Table 7–45
Prediction of Comprehension for Animatic and Storyboard Commercials
(N = 293)

	Multiple R	Beta[a]
Front-end impact (factor 8)	.21	.17
Time until identification (factor 3)	.26	.15
Indirect comparison (factor 19)	.30	− .14
Substantive supers (factor 24)	.32	.13

Multiple R = .32
R^2 = .10
Adjusted R^2 = .09
[a]Standardized regression coefficients, all significant at the .05 level.

Table 7–46
Prediction of Persuasion for Animatic and
Storyboard Commercials
(N = 293)

	Multiple R	Beta[a]
Brand-differentiating message	.24	.22
Convenience in use (factor 21)	.28	.13
Product reminder (factor 20)	.31	− .13
Brand prominence (factor 7)	.33	.14
Cast (factor 5)	.35	− .13
User satisfaction (factor 9)	.37	.11

Multiple R = .37
R^2 = .14
Adjusted R^2 = .12
[a]Standardized regression coefficients, all significant at the .05 level.

ory-related devices. Substantive supers and number of on-screen characters have a positive impact on the recall of storyboard and animatic commercials, while they have the opposite effect in live commercials.

Brand-Differentiating Messages and Other Commercial Executional Elements

Given the pervasive importance of a brand-differentiating claim, it is useful to examine the relationships between the presence or absence of such a message and other executional elements. Table 7–47 provides the frequency with which various other elements occur in commercials with and without brand-differentiating messages. All reported differences and correlations are statistically significant. Commercials providing sensory information, information on results of using the product, product demonstrations, music, and background casts are less likely to make a brand-differentiating claim. Commercials with brand-differentiating claims are more likely to accompany family-branded products, competitor comparisons, information on attributes and ingredients, product introduction early in the commercial, and brand prominence. It is also noteworthy that the commercials for new products are more likely to make a brand-differentiating claim than commercials for established products.

Table 7–47
Differences in Executional Variables between Commercials with and without Brand-Differentiating Message

	No Brand-Differentiating Message	Brand-Differentiating Message Present	r
Sensory information	52	45	
Results of using	59	51	
New product	40	60	
Family branded	28	36	
Setting directly relevant	70	59	
No setting	16	27	
Attributes/ingredients	50	61	
Enjoying life	13	6	
Modern contemporary	29	20	
Direct comparison	7	16	
Indirect comparison	24	34	
Demonstration in use	65	54	
Mood/image dominant	36	25	
Music present	47	37	
Music major element	15	7	
Female principal character	65	56	
Background cast	32	20	
Biserial correlation of brand-differentiating message and:			
Time until product category identification			−.08
Time product is on screen			.10
Time brand name or logo is on screen			.13
Number of vignettes			−.08
Number of on-screen characters			−.17

New Products and Executional Factors

New and established products differ with respect to the frequency with which certain executional devices are employed. New products are more likely not only to have a brand-differentiating message but also to offer information on product benefits, product attributes/ingredients, research, and convenience of the product in use and to make indirect comparisons. Commercials for new products are also more likely to devote more time to the product and to have continuity of action. They are less likely to employ a large cast, to offer information on user satisfaction, use auditory memory devices, and include graphics (table 7–48).

Table 7–48
Executional Factors Differentiating Commercials for New versus Established Products

	New	Established	Overall Mean
Brand-differentiating message	.12	− .34	− .12
Product benefits (factor 2)	.19	− .16	.00
Product attributes/components/ ingredients (factor 4)	.19	− .16	.00
Cast (factor 5)	− .17	.15	.00
Brand prominence (factor 7)	.14	− .13	− .01
User satisfaction (factor 9)	− .09	.08	.00
Auditory memory devices (factor 12)	− .14	.15	.01
Continuity (factor 16)	.10	− .09	.00
Serious/graphics (factor 17)	− .07	.07	.00
Indirect comparison (factor 19)	.08	− .08	.00
Convenience in use (factor 21)	.10	− .12	− .01
Research (factor 23)	.09	− .10	− .01

Note: All differences are significant at the .05 level.

8
Discussion and Conclusions: Need for a New Research Paradigm

Shanteau (1983) suggests that advertising may not be very important in the larger scheme of things. Achenbaum (1972) concludes that while consumers may be willing to try new products as a result of advertising, "consumers are choosing brands based on positive product experience regardless of advertising" (p. 10), and previous studies of advertising effects have found that relatively little of the variation in any particular measure of advertising performance can be attributed to specific executional factors. In the present study, not more than 15 percent of the variance of recall, comprehension, or persuasion was specifically accounted for by executional factors. While not overwhelming, the amount of variance accounted for by execution is certainly nontrivial. Further, this variance is produced by a single exposure to an ad. In a highly competitive marketplace, a 15 percent advantage may mean the difference between success and failure.

The single most important advertising executional factor related to the persuasiveness of a commercial is the presence of a brand-differentiating message. The finding is new, but the idea is not. Borden (1942) concluded that effective advertising provides a basis for differentiating products. The creative philosophies of well-known advertising professionals such as Rosser Reeves and David Ogilvy have emphasized product differentiation through the development of unique selling propositions and brand images. It is surprising that no published advertising research has even considered the influence of brand-differentiating claims. This oversight can probably be attributed to the dominant research paradigms employed in much prior research that emphasize the study of cognitive responses to an advertising stimulus using traditional laboratory research methods. Product choice behavior as the principal function of advertising has been widely neglected until recently (Shanteau 1983; Estes 1980).

The neglect of choice behavior in the study of advertising is clearly manifest in the choice of measures used in prior research. These measures have seldom included actual choice behavior. More often these measures have included recall and comprehension measures, attitudinal measures, intention measures, and ratings of relevance, believability, numbers and types of cognitions, and likability. The assumption implicit in the use of such measures is that a strong link exists between these measures and product choice. The results of the present study suggest that whatever links may exist are influenced by many factors. Different elements of the advertising stimulus appear to influence different measures of performance, and the performance measures have complex relationships. The set of factors that influence recall are not identical to those that influence persuasion, and the nature of the influence of those factors varies under different conditions.

It is time to shift the focus of research on advertising effectiveness to modifying or maintaining choice behavior. The primary long-term role of advertising is to persuade. Recall and comprehension appear to be important mediators of persuasion but are not the primary functions of advertising. Industry practice has already begun to shift to an emphasis on persuasion measures (Gibson 1983; Ross 1982).

The remainder of this chapter is concerned with interpreting the results of the present study and the implications of those results for future research on advertising effectiveness. Many of the results fit neatly within an information theory framework, and potential avenues for research within that framework are discussed in subsequent sections of the chapter.

Recapitulation of Results

While the single most important executional determinant of both recall and persuasion was the presence of a brand-differentiating message, the relationship of brand-differentiating message and persuasion was a function of the level of recall attained by the commercial and characteristics of the product being advertised. At higher levels of recall, brand-differentiating messages account for twice the variance accounted for at lower levels of recall. In addition, brand-differentiating messages appear to account for more variance in persuasion among established products with a higher market share of users.

Differences in the levels of related recall and persuasion appear to be accounted for by two sets of elements: (1) brand performance characteristics such as brand-differentiating claims and convenience of the product in use and (2) attention and memory factors such as humor, auditory memory devices, brand prominence in the commercial, front-end impact, and brand sign-off.

Recall, comprehension, and persuasion appear to operate more independently for established product commercials, but these processes are less separable for new products. The new product response process appears to be much more recall driven. The pattern of relationships between executional factors and measures of effectiveness for new product commercials is similar to the pattern for all products that have a low share of users.

The results of the present study suggest that a variety of executional devices may enhance recall and comprehension. These include attention and memory variables such as the use of humor, auditory memory devices, brand sign-off, front-end impact, and amount of time devoted to the product within the commercial and brand performance factors such as the use of a brand-differentiating message, information concerning convenience in use, and product benefits. Other factors appear to interfere with recall and comprehension, such as company identification, information about product attributes and components, and information on nutrition and health. This finding is consistent with the findings of Jacoby, Chestnut, and Silberman (1977), in six separate studies, that most consumers do not attend to or comprehend nutrition information when making decisions about food products. This suggests that advertisers should exercise caution when using attributes/ingredients information in commercials to make sure information is relevant and the presentation interesting.

Contrary to the findings of prior research about the lack of information in commercials (Bauer and Greyser 1968; Resnik and Stern 1977), the present study found television commercials on average to be reasonably informative. Each commercial provided an average of four distinct categories of information. For new products the average was five pieces of information; the only difference from established product advertising was information that the product is new.

The findings of the present study are consistent with the results of previous studies cited in chapter 2. The importance of humor, product demonstrations, memory devices, and time devoted to the product is consistent with previous research. However, some differences are noted. For example, McEwen and Leavitt (1976) found front-end impact (opening suspense) negatively related to recall. The present findings indicate a positive relationship, but this relationship is mediated by whether or not the product is new. Front-end impact tends to be important for new product commercials, but it is not a significant predictor of recall for established products.

Why Brand Differentiation Is Important: An Information Theory Perspective

The results of the present study concerning the importance of an explicit brand-differentiating claim affirm the creative philosophy of advertising articulated by Rosser Reeves (1961) about the importance of creating a unique selling proposition for every advertised product. The role of advertising is to communicate something specific, unique to the product, and important to consumers. Still, what is needed is a theoretical framework that builds on this finding.

Stewart and Haley (1983) have suggested that a primary function of marketing communication should be to suggest a basis for consumer choice. Choice rules tell the prospective buyer how to choose a particular brand (Percy and Rossiter 1980). While choice rules pertain to the total product category, they can be used by brand advertisers to encourage consumers to use a choice rule that favors the company's brand (Wright and Barbour 1977). Unfortunately, choice rules are a neglected phenomenon in empirical advertising research (Rossiter and Percy 1983), probably because choice has been so infrequently studied.

Nelson (1974) suggests that the primary function of advertising is to inform. He identifies four informative functions of advertising:

Relating a brand to a product function,

Implying that a brand is a better buy than other brands,

Providing direct information that will help the consumer rank brands by their utility and/or reduce the risk associated with the decision to purchase the product,

Reminding the consumer of the product, thereby reducing the cost to the consumer of remembering the brand.

Relating a brand to a product function is necessary, particularly for a new or relatively unknown product, to suggest why a product might be purchased and the relevant set of reasonable substitutes. Where the product performs a unique function, a basis for differentiation, this type of information alone may be sufficient to prompt choice. However, few products perform unique functions. More typical is the situation in which a consumer must select a product from a larger set of products that perform the same function. In such circumstances, the consumer must identify a basis for choice among the alternatives. Advertising that implys the product is a better buy or that provides information that helps the consumer rank brands, identifies a basis for choice among alternatives. Product reminders are for established products for which the choice rules are already well established, and the function of advertising is to reinforce or reinstate past habits.

Wright (1981) has suggested that what is most likely to be retained from broadcast advertising is a problem frame, a way of thinking about the purchase decision. This includes the set of attributes to be considered when making the purchase decision. The presence of a brand-differentiating claim is one form of problem framing, since it identifies a relevant dimension along which product alternatives differ. Among a relatively homogeneous set of alternatives, any qualitative difference may be sufficient to provide a basis for choice among some customers. Zeleny (1982) has argued, and offers some empirical support for, the proposition that decision makers will seek additional attributes to differentiate alternatives that are otherwise identical (or nearly identical) on an initial set of attributes. Under such circumstances, the presence of any claimed differentiating characteristics, even when not relevant to the performance or function of the product, will provide a basis for a decision that cannot otherwise be made except by random selection.

A brand-differentiating claim can be made with or without any basis for that claim, although most commercials that employ such a claim are communicating a real and demonstrable product difference. It is not clear from the data in the present study that the mere claim of uniqueness without credible support will produce higher levels of persuasion, although this is probably a hypothesis worth testing. Other things being equal, any perceived difference among alternatives may serve as the basis for choice.

Support for the decision rule hypothesis offered here may also be found in the literature on the economics of advertising. A substantial body of literature suggests that advertising may, in one manner or another, act as a signal of quality to the marketplace (Kihlstrom and Riordan 1984; Wolinsky 1981, 1983; Klein and Leffler 1981; Johnsen 1976; Nelson 1970, 1974, 1978). Indeed, it has been argued (Nelson 1978; Kihlstrom and Riordan 1984) that advertising alone, in the absence of direct information about product qualities within the advertising execution, may be sufficient to signal a difference in product quality, provided a market mechanism exists that produces a positive relationship between product quality and advertising expenditures. In such cases consumers use observable information (for example, amount of advertising) to infer quality. The consumer, in the absence of any other differentiating characteristics of the product alternatives, will use differences in the amount of advertising as the basis for choice.

To accept the hypotheses offered here, it is necessary to broaden the definition of product quality. While products may well differ along measurable dimensions of quality of performance, many products do not differ perceptibly. Consumers will always find a basis for a choice among product alternatives on any given occasion. In recognition of the consumer's need for a basis for choice, firms may seek to offer such a basis to the consumer, whether that basis is related strictly to product function or not. By this definition, quality differences represent any basis for discriminating between product alternatives.

The analysis of the bases for discrimination among alternatives leads to an information theory paradigm of advertising research. Within this paradigm, information is defined in terms of the reduction of uncertainty or ambiguity in a choice situation. The smallest unit of information, a bit, is the minimum amount of information required to discriminate between two alternatives. Such a definition implies that there is no information value in communicating a product attribute that exhibits no variation among alternatives. A brand-differentiating claim must introduce meaningful variation among alternatives, but it need not be directly related to unique product functions (for example, the only product approved for use by the U.S. Olympic team). When products are perceived to be very similar, any basis for differentiation, whether or not related to product performance, may represent the basis for choice. When a particular brand-differentiating message involves an attribute salient to product performance or function, it is likely to be stronger than a competing differentiating message that is unrelated to product performance. Many brands in a product category may make brand-differentiating claims, but not all of them will be equally effective. Brands that make no brand-differentiating claims in their advertising, however, are the most vulnerable.

Relationships between Recall, Product Characteristics, Persuasion, and Brand Differentiation

The foregoing discussion suggests why brand differentiation was found to be important in the present study but sheds little light on why level of related recall and product characteristics such as stage in life cycle and share of users mediates the relationship between persuasion and brand differentiation. Research on cognition, as well as an understanding of the advertising environment, is useful for understanding this phenomenon. For a brand-differentiating message to have an impact on consumer choice, it must first be received by the viewer. Within the cluttered and distracting environment of broadcast advertising, viewer reception requires obtaining viewer attention. This may be accomplished either through the use of attention-capturing devices in a particular advertising execution or through repetition of the execution over time. The present study did not afford the opportunity to examine directly the effects of message repetition (for example, campaign effects) since the measure of persuasion was obtained after a single exposure. The present study did examine the effects of brand-differentiating claim on persuasion among commercials achieving high and low recall. In cases where recall of the commercial was high, there was greater opportunity for the brand-differentiating message to be received and processed by the viewer. The presence of a brand-differentiating message has a considerably greater impact on choice in those cases where the commercial was better remembered.

The influence of product life cycle (new versus established) and level of prechoice (a surrogate for market share) on the relationship between persuasion and brand-differentiating message is also the result of differences in the degree to which the brand-differentiating message has been received and processed by the viewer. Viewers of a new product commercial have had but one opportunity to learn the basis of differentiation. For established products, the brand-differentiating message may have been learned from exposure to other commercials for the same product and from actual use of the product. It is less important that consumers of established products be able to recall a specific commercial execution to be persuaded. Thus, recall is a much stronger mediating influence on new product persuasion. A similar explanation may account for the mediating influence of prechoice. Brands with higher shares of current users are already better known than those established brands with lower prechoice levels. Thus, general level of brand awareness should work to facilitate the processing of the brand-differentiating message for high prechoice brands even when recall of the specific execution is not high.

Lingle and Ostrom (1981) suggest that meaning is abstracted from stimulus material and often stored separately in memory from the stimulus information. Inferences and the facts supporting those inferences may be stored separately. The previously stored meaning of prior information may act to organize new information in a manner that culls irrelevant information from a persuasive communication. Thus, it is possible that once a brand-differentiating message (problem frame) is stored, it may influence decisions even in the absence of recall of the specific communication in which it was learned or reinforced. When there has not been such prior storage, the entire communication is the vehicle for information organization and influence on choice. This is probably the reason why recall and persuasion for new product commercials are more highly associated. For established products, different executional factors appeared to be the primary influencers of recall and persuasion. The only positive factor significantly influencing persuasion for established products is the presence of a brand-differentiating claim.

Also useful for understanding the present results are the findings of Petty (1977b) and Raj (1982). The persuasion measure employed in the present study was taken soon after exposure to a television commercial embedded within a television program and other commercials. Raj found that increased levels of advertising had the strongest impact on highly loyal consumers (those selecting the same brand on at least 50 percent of their purchase occasions). Little effect of advertising was observed on low loyalty customers (those selecting the same brand on less than 30 percent of all purchase occasions). Switchers change brands routinely, so only brand loyals are particularly affected. These results are consistent with the present findings that more of the variance in persuasion could be accounted for among higher prechoice products than lower prechoice products. In the Raj study, a particular commercial was observed to have its impact on high loyalty consumers by increasing the purchase rate of the product advertised if it was already the product of choice or generating switching from another product, to which prior loyalty had existed, to the advertised product. The persuasion measure used in the present study is a switching measure and is thus likely to be affected primarily by advertising shifting purchase from one product to another.

Petty (1977b) identified the mechanism by which this change may occur. He suggests that two different types of persuasion may occur as a result of communication. Temporary shifts of attitude or behavior may occur without cognitive processing as a result of exposure to what Petty calls *persuasion cues*. Enduring changes are hypothesized to require processing of message content. Since it is unlikely that much cognitive processing occurs in response to broadcast ads (Wright 1981), the changes in persuasion obtained in the present analysis are probably most attributable to temporary shifts in response to a persuasive cue—in this case, a change in the problem frame suggested by a brand-differentiating claim. The data concerning the validity of the persuasion measure used in the present study would suggest that shifts in response to a persuasive cue may be relatively more enduring than Petty's original hypothesis suggests. Indeed, when the brand-differentiating message provides the only basis for choice among otherwise homogeneous goods, and the message is reinforced on a regular basis, such changes may endure for long periods of time. Whether such changes can become permanent with time and in the presence of other competing persuasive cues is an empirical question.

Note on Partial Replication

During the course of the larger study reported in this book, a proprietary database of more than 200 television commercials was made available to the authors for purposes of replication. Since this dataset was considerably smaller and represented a somewhat smaller set of product categories, a complete replication was not possible. Further, the proprietary nature of the dataset prevents full disclosure of the results. However, two points are worth noting from this partial replication. The major results of the larger study held up remarkably well on replication. Brand-differentiating message was confirmed as the most important factor for predicting persuasion. Recall level and prechoice manifest the same mediating effects on the relationship between persuasion and the presence of a brand-differentiating message. Unfortunately, the replication dataset was not adequate to allow for a new versus established product analysis. Various attention/memory devices also manifest similar relationships to those manifest in the larger study. However, not all relationships of individual executional elements exhibited the same relationships to recall, comprehension, and persuasion reported for the larger study. This suggests that caution be exercised in interpreting any result for specific executional devices.

Some of the differences between the larger and smaller studies are directly attributable to the problem raised by Fishbein and Ajzen (1981) that there is a confounding of information content and executional devices. In some cases executional devices carry product information and even provide a basis for product differentiation. In a descriptive study like this one, it is impossible to control for such confounding.

A larger replication of the present study is planned, but a sufficiently large number of commercials will not be available for analysis for at least 2 years. This second, larger replication will, in due course, be reported.

Directions for Future Research

The present study raises some questions for future research, suggests a need for a different focus in advertising research, and offers a theoretical framework that should be tested. The study demonstrates that the relationship between recall and persuasion is not as simplistic as assumed. While there is a positive association between the two measures, the strength of that association is relatively modest and appears to differ under various conditions (for example, new and established products). Future research efforts would be more insightful if the focus were on measures of persuasion, or behavior change, rather than exclusively on cognitive measures such as recall or attitude change. This is not to suggest that these other measures are unimportant but that they should be treated as intervening variables influencing the primary measure of consumer choice.

The present results have implications for the development and refinement of measures of advertising effectiveness. The nature of measures of recall, comprehension, and persuasion, and the relationships among these measures, appear to differ with both level of prechoice and recall. Relationships also differ for new versus established products. This suggests that these measures may be tapping somewhat different processes, or different aspects of a dynamic process. Recall and persuasion may not mean the same thing for new products as they do for established products. For new products, recall and persuasion appear to be integral to the same process, while for established products they appear to be more independent. The nature of these measures requires elaboration in future research.

The present study is among the very few to use measures of demonstrated reliability and validity. Future research should pay greater attention to measures development. No testable theory of advertising can emerge without first establishing the validity of operational measures of advertising effects. Reviews by Stewart et al. (1985a and b) have called attention to the need for measure validation and for attention to the generalizability of measures. The present study used measures obtained in a situation similar to the typical broadcast advertising situation. As Shanteau (1983, p. 158) points out, "Results obtained in the traditional [cognitive] research environments cannot be simply generalized to the advertising situation." Future research must be carried out in settings more nearly similar to a realistic advertising environment. This does not preclude laboratory research, but it does suggest the form such laboratory research might take. The foregoing comments suggest methodological changes for research in the future. There are also important substantive issues raised in the present study that require further research.

There is some empirical evidence to support the hypothesis offered that prior awareness of a product may mediate the relationship between advertising execution, recall, and persuasion (Holman and Hecker 1983). This hypothesis could not be tested with the current database. An examination of prior awareness of product, measured, perhaps, by top-of-mind recall, and its influence on both the recall and persuasion performances of test commercials would be a fruitful endeavor.

Further work on the nature of brand-differentiating messages would be particularly worthwhile. An understanding of how competing differentiating claims are processed by consumers and the circumstances influencing the salience of different types of brand-differentiating claims would add much to the understanding of how advertising works. An understanding of the individual processes underlying the aggregate results of the present study would be very useful.

A shift in the focus of research from the effects of specific executional devices to consideration of the information content carried by such devices is desirable. In a large study like the one reported here, the type of effect and information confounding suggested by Fishbein and Ajzen (1981) is less likely to occur. In smaller studies it is critical to control for information content. The present study would suggest that certain devices—humor and auditory memory devices—have attentional effects quite apart from information content. The presence of a brand-differentiating message, however, appears to have both informational content and a memory-facilitating effect. It is important that future research come to grips with what is actually being studied—that is, what it is in the stimulus that is producing the effect on the dependent variable.

The present study has not examined the effects of repeated exposures or changes in behavior over time. Future research should explore the impact of multiple exposures, multiple purchase occasions, and the effects of competitive advertising.

Conclusion

Descriptive studies usually raise more questions than they answer. The present study is no exception. Descriptive studies often provide directions for future research by suggesting what is and is not relevant for further study. The impact of the presence of a brand-differentiating claim in the present study offers a direction for future work. The mediating influences of recall and product characteristics on the relationship between persuasion and brand-differentiating message are intriguing. The present results suggest that recall and persuasion, while related, are fundamentally different measures, that one is not a substitute for another, and that the relationship between these measures is not simple.

The danger of any study of executional factors in advertising is that results will be interpreted at face value without understanding the more complex processes at work to produce the effect. We hope that a contribution of the present study is to point out higher-order relationships than are evident from looking at only a few things one at a time. Bivariate and multivariate results have been presented since each provides an insight into the nature of advertising execution. Whether the study makes a substantial contribution to understanding the effects of advertising, only time will tell.

Appendix A:
Codebook

Information Content

(D001) **Price:** Refers to the amount the consumer must pay for the product or service; this may be in absolute terms, like a suggested retail price, or relative terms, like a 10 percent off sale.

(D002) **Value:** Refers to some combination of price and quality or quantity, as in more x for the money, better quality at a low price, the best value for the dollar.

(D003) **Quality:** Refers to how good the product or service is; may refer to craftsmanship and/or attention during manufacture, use of quality (better, best) ingredients or components, length of time to produce or create the product.

(D004) **Economy/savings:** Refers to saving money or time either in the original purchase or in the use of the product relative to other products in the category.

(D005) **Dependability/reliability/durability:** Information concerning how long the product will last without repair, service records, and so on.

(D006) **Sensory information** (taste, fragrance, touch, comfort): Information concerning a sensory experience: "smells April fresh," "tastes homemade," "feels silky smooth," "smooth taste," "luxurious comfort."

(D007) **Aesthetic claims** (styling, color): Information concerning appearance, classic beauty, and so on of the product either when purchased or when prepared in final form.

(D008) **Components, contents, or ingredients:** What went into the making or manufacture of the product—for example, "contains lanolin," "made with pudding." These contents should be in the product purchased, not ingredients added to the product by the consumer in preparation for use.

(D009) **Availability:** Any information concerning the place(s) the consumer may purchase or otherwise obtain the product—for example, "available in supermarkets," "look for it in the dairy section." May also refer to places where the product is not available—for example, "not available in all areas."

(D010) **Packaging:** Information about the packaging of the product—for example, "look for the package with the red spoon," "look for our special two in one package," "the package is reusable," "in the convenient one serving package."

(D011) **Guarantees or warranty:** Refers to any information concerning the presence of a guarantee or warranty, including but not restricted to money back offers, offers to repair or service the product in the event of problems, or offers to replace the product if the consumer is dissatisfied or has a problem.

(D012) **Safety:** Information concerning the safety of the product—for example, "has a built-in cut-off switch," "nontoxic," "won't harm delicate hair."

(D013) **Nutrition/health:** Information concerning the nutritional or health-related characteristics of the product—for example, "fortified with vitamin D," "the formula doctors recommend," "relieves iron-poor blood."

(D014) **Independent research results:** Information offered about tests of the product or of product users that were carried out by an identified individual or organization other than the company manufacturing or distributing the product, such as Underwriter's Laboratory, a leading university, or the U.S. government. Such tests may concern objective product characteristics ("lasts twice as long") or may be related to user preferences ("preferred by two-thirds of the people surveyed").

(D015) **Company-sponsored research results:** Information about tests of the product or users of the product that were carried out by the company manufacturing or distributing the product—for example, the Pepsi challenge.

(D016) **Research results from unidentified source:** Information about tests of the product or users of the product when the source of the test results is not identified.

(D017)   **New uses:** Refers to any information about a new way to use an established product—for example, "use X brand paper cups for sorting and storing nuts and bolts," "new recipes," "use Y baking soda to deodorize refrigerator."

(D018)   **Company image or reputation:** Refers to any information about the image or reputation of the company that manufactures or distributes the product—for example, "we've been in business longer than anyone else," "we try harder," "the other guys," "babies are our business."

(D019)   **Results of using (either tangible or intangible):** Any information concerning the outcomes associated with the use of the product. These outcomes may be in a positive form—"gives hair bounce," "makes you feel healthier,"—or a negative form—"won't yellow floors."

(D020)   **User's satisfaction/dedication/loyalty:** Refers to any information concerning users' satisfaction, preference for the brand, or length of time consumer has used the advertised product—for example, "I'd never give up my Tide," "I've always used . . . ."

(D021)   **Superiority claim:** Information that claims the advertised product is better than competitive products or an older version of the advertised product in some particular way(s).

(D022)   **Convenience in use:** Information concerning the ease with which the product may be obtained, prepared, used, or disposed of.

(D023)   **Special offer or event:** Information concerning special events such as sales, contests, two-for-one deals, premiums, or rebates to occur for a specified limited time.

(D024)   **New product or new/improved product features:** Refers to any information concerning a new product introduction, new components, ingredients, features, or characteristics of an existing product or an improvement (qualitative or quantitative) in any feature, component, ingredient, or characteristic of an existing product— for example, "new and improved," "now with 50 percent less sugar," "new, milder . . .," "new, stronger . . . ," "now with built-in flash."

(D025)   **Use occasion:** Information that clearly suggests an appropriate use occasion or situation for the product—for example, "buy film for the Christmas season," "enjoy Jello at a birthday party," "the beer for special occasions."

(D026) **Characteristics or image of users:** Refers to any information concerning the type(s) of individual(s) who might use the advertised product—for example, "for the young at heart," "for the busy career woman."

Brand and Product Identification

(D027) **No product:** No product is identified in the commercial.

Single product: A single product is the focus of the commercial.

Multiple products: The commercial presents two or more distinct product lines—for example, Keebler Cookies, Keebler Crackers.

(D028) **Double-branded product:** Does the product have two brand names—for example, Keebler Rich 'n Chips, Canon AE1, Ford Fairmont?

(D029) **Identification of company manufacturing and/or distributing the product:** Is the company manufacturing or distributing the product identified in the commercial, either as part of the brand name (Ford Fairmont) or explicitly ("another fine product from General Foods")? (Note: Do not include copyright identifiers as company identifiers.)

(D030) **Visual brand sign-off:** Is the brand name, package, or other obvious identifier of the product visible as the commercial ends?

(D031) **Auditory sign-off:** Is the brand name repeated within the last 3 seconds of the commercial?

Congruence of Commercial Elements

Brand Name Reinforces Product Message

(D032) 1. Brand name provides no product information (Tide, Duz, Cheer, Gleem);

2. Brand name reinforces a product benefit somewhat (Dove, Caress, Life-saver Radial, Firestone 721 Tires, Anyday Pantyliners);

3. Brand name states exactly (or almost) what product is or will do (Bonz Dog Biscuits) or is by strong reputation clearly identified with the product category or particular benefit (Kodak Instamatic Camera).

Setting

(D033) Setting not related to normal product use or purchase (for example, car on top of mountain peak);

(D034) Setting unrelated to product use but somehow relevant to product performance (for example, demonstration of Timex watch strapped to bottom of speedboat, pick-up truck driving up a pile of boulders);

(D035) Setting directly related to normal product use or purchase situation (for example, car in showroom, driveway);

(D036) No setting.

Visual Devices

(D037) **Scenic beauty:** Does the commercial present striking scenes of natural beauty (mountains, flowing streams) at some point?

(D038) **Beauty of one or more principal characters:** Does the commercial present one or more strikingly beautify people?

(D039) **Ugliness of one or more principal characters:** Does the commercial present one or more strikingly ugly characters?

(D040) **Graphic displays:** Does the commercial use graphic displays or charts as part of its presentation? Such graphics may be computer generated.

(D041) **Surrealistic visuals:** Does the commercial present unreal visuals, distorted visuals, fantastic scenes like a watch floating through outer space?

(D042) **Substantive supers:** A superscript (words on the screen) used to reinforce some characteristic of the product or a part of the commercial message—for example, "50% stronger," "3 out of 4 doctors recommend."

(D043) **Visual tagline:** A visually presented statement of new information at the end of the commercial; for example, the screen shows the name of participating dealers or another product that was not the focus of the commercial shown. Corporate logos or slogans do not qualify.

(D044) **Use of visual memory device:** Any device shown that reinforces product benefits, the product name, or the message delivered by the commercial—for example, time release capsules bouncing in the air, the word *Jello* spelled out with Jello Gelatin, piece of sun in Polaroid commercials.

Auditory Devices

(D045) **Memorable rhymes, slogans, or mnemonic devices:** Nonmusical rhymes or other mnemonics (memory aid devices) may be incorporated in lyric of a song, but must also stand alone, apart from music—for example, "You're in good hands with Allstate," "Get a piece of the rock".

(D046) **Unusual sound effects:** Out of place, unusual, or bizarre use of sound—for example, the sound of a jackhammer as someone eats a pretzel.

(D047) **Spoken tagline:** A statement at the end of the commercial that presents new information, usually unrelated to the principal focus of the commercial—for example, "And try new lime flavor too."

Promises, Appeals, or Selling Propositions

(D048) **Attributes or ingredients as main message:** A major focus of the commercial is to communicate something about how the product is made (for example, care in manufacturing) or ingredients (for example, the only toothpaste with stannous fluoride).

(D049) **Product performance or benefits as main message:** A major focus of the commercial is to communicate what the product does (for example, shinier tub, fresher breath, whiter teeth) or how to use it.

(D050) **Psychological or subjective benefits of product ownership:** A major focus of the commercial is to communicate hidden or nonprovable benefits of having/using the product (for example, "you'll be more popular, sexier, more confident").

(D051) **Product reminder as main message:** The product or package is the primary message rather than any specific attribute or benefit of use.

(D052) **Sexual appeal:** Main focus of commercial is on sexual cues.

(D053) **Comfort appeals:** Main focus of commercial is on cues appealing to creature comforts (soft chairs, cool climate).

(D054) **Safety appeals:** Main focus of commercial is on cues appealing to being free from fear or physical danger.

(D055) **Enjoyment appeals:** Main focus of commercial is on cues about enjoying life to the fullest, having good food and drink, and so on.

(D056) **Welfare appeals:** Main focus is on caring or providing for others (for example, gift giving).

(D057) **Social approval:** Main focus of commercial is on belonging, winning friends, obtaining approval of others.

(D058) **Self-esteem or self-image:** Main focus of commercial is on feeling better about oneself, improving oneself, being a better person.

(D059) **Achievement:** Main focus of commercial is on obtaining superiority over others, getting ahead, winning.

(D060) **Excitement, sensation, variety:** Main focus of commercial is on adding excitement, thrills, variety to life, avoiding boredom.

Commercial Tone or Atmosphere

(D061) **Cute/adorable**

(D062) **Hard sell**

(D063) **Warm and caring**

(D064) **Modern/contemporary**

(D065) **Wholesome/healthy**

(D066) **Technological/futuristic**

(D067) **Conservative/traditional**

(D068) **Old Fashioned/nostalgic**

(D069) **Happy/fun-loving**

(D070) **Cool/laid-back**

(D071) **Somber/serious**

(D072) **Uneasy/tense/irritated**

(D073) **Relaxed/comfortable**

(D074) **Glamorous**

(D075)   **Humorous**

(D076)   **Suspenseful**

(D077)   **Rough/rugged**

Comparisons

(D078)   **Direct comparison with other products:** A competitor is identified by name. May also be a direct comparison with an old version of the product advertised.

(D079)   **Indirect comparison with other products:** A comparison is made between the advertised product and a competitor, but the competitor is not named.

(D080)   **Puffery, or unsubstantiated claim:** Product is declared best, better, finest without identification of dimension or attribute.

Commercial Structures

(D081)   **Front-end impact:** The first 10 seconds of the commercial creates suspense, questions, surprise, drama, or something that otherwise gains attention.

(D082)   **Surprise or suspense in middle of commercial:** Something surprising, dramatic, or suspenseful occurs in the middle of the commercial.

(D083)   **Surprise or suspense at closing:** Commercial ends with a surprise, an unexpected event, suspense, or drama.

(D084)   **Unusual setting or situation:** Product is in setting not normally associated with product purchase or use—for example, a car on top of a mountain, a contemporary wine in ancient Greece.

(D085)   **Humorous closing:** Commercial ends with a joke, pun, witticism, or slapstick.

(D086)   **Blind lead-in:** No identification of product until the end of the commercial.

(D087)   **Message in middle (doughnut):** Music and/or action at the start and close of commercial with announcer copy in the middle—for example, Green Giant commercials.

Commercial Format

(D088) **Vignettes:** A series of two or more stories that could stand alone; no continuing storyline but several independent stories (which may convey the same message). Multiple interviews would be an example. Has no continuity of action.

(D089) **Continuity of action:** Commercial has a single storyline throughout with an obvious beginning, middle, and end; a common theme, character, or issue ties the whole commercial together from beginning to end. This may be an interview with a single individual, slice of life, or any other format that involves continuity of action.

(D090) **Slice of life:** An interplay between two or more people that portrays a conceivable real-life situation. There is continuity of action.

(D091) **Testimonial by product user:** One or more individuals recounts his or her satisfaction with the product advertised or the results of using the product advertised—for example, Bill Cosby for Jello Pudding, Henry Fonda for Life Savers.

(D092) **Endorsement by celebrity or authority:** One or more individuals (or organizations) advocates or recommends the product but does not claim personal use or satisfaction—for example, Karl Malden for American Express.

(D093) **Announcement:** Commercial's format is that of a newscast or sportscast, sales announcement.

(D094) **Demonstration of product in use or by analogy:** A demonstration of the product in use—for example, a man shaving in a commercial for shaving lather, women applying makeup, no pantylines in pantyhose commercial. A demonstration of the use of the product, benefit, or product characteristic by an analogy or device rather than actual demonstration, as in the case of dipping chalk into a beaker of fluoride to demonstrate how fluoride is to be absorbed by teeth.

(D095) **Demonstration of results of using the product:** Demonstration of the outcome of using the product—for example, shining floors, bouncing hair.

(D096) **Comedy or satire:** The commercial is written as a comedy, parody, or satire. Not only is humor an element of the commercial, but also the commercial is written to be funny.

(D097) **Animation/cartoon/rotoscope:** The entire commercial or some substantial part of the commercial is animated; for example, the Green Giant opening is always a cartoon followed by real life in middle or the Keebler Elves. A rotoscope is a combination of real life and animation on the screen at the same time—for example, the Trix rabbit.

(D098) **Photographic stills:** The use of photographic stills in part of the commercial. These may be product shots, settings, or models.

(D099) **Creation of mood or image as dominant element:** An attempt to create a desire for the product, without offering a specific product claim, by appealing to the viewer's emotional/sensory involvement. The primary thrust of the commercial is the creation of a feeling or mood.

(D100) **Commercial written as serious drama:** The commercial is written as a stage play, melodrama, or tragedy.

(D101) **Fantasy, exaggeration, or surrealism as dominant element:** The use of animation or other visual device instead of a realistic treatment to suspend disbelief or preclude literal translation on the part of the viewer.

(D102) **Problem and solution (before/after presentation):** An attempt to define or show a problem, then indicate how the product eliminates or reduces the problem—for example, "ring around the collar."

(D103) **Interview (person on the street or elsewhere):** An interview (questions and answers) is a primary vehicle in the commercial for Rolaids, "How do you spell relief?"

(D104) **Camera involves audience in situation:** Use of camera as eyes of viewer. Camera creates participation in commercial.

(D105) **New wave (product graphics):** Use of posterlike visuals, fast cuts, high symbolism as in Diet Pepsi, RC 100, Lincoln-Mercury (Lynx), Magnavox (with Leonard Nimoy).

Production Characteristics and Quality

(D106) **Number of words in commercial:** The average 30-second commercial has 60 to 70 words in it. Does the commercial clearly have fewer than this number (*few*), about this number (*average*), or obviously more than this number (*many*)? Words in songs count as words. For commercials longer or shorter than 30 seconds, use the ratio of length of commercial to 30 seconds to determine number of words. Codes: 1 = no words, 2 = few, 3 = average, 4 = many.

(D107) **Visual pace of commercial (number of camera cuts):** The average 30-second commercial has 6 to 8 camera cuts. Indicate whether the commercial has a *fewer, average, many more* scene changes. For commercials longer or shorter than 30 seconds, use the ratio of length of commercial to 30 seconds to determine the number of scene changes. Codes: 1 = fewer, 2 = average, 3 = many.

Music and Dancing

(D108) **Music:** Is music present in the commercial in any form?

(D109) **Music as major element:** Do the lyrics of the music used in the commercial carry a product message—for example, "Have it your way . . ." "I'm a Pepper . . ."?

(D110) **Music creates mood (versus background only):** Music contributes to the creation of a mood or emotion—for example, suspense, sensuality.

(D111) **Dancing:** Do cast members dance in the commercial?

(D112) **Musical and dance extravaganza:** Is there a large cast (more than five) that engages in singing or dancing during a significant portion of the commercial, like in the Pepper commercial?

(D113) **Adaptation of well-known music:** Is music recognized popular, classical, country and western tune—for example, "Anticipation"?

(D114) **Recognized continuing musical theme:** Is music clearly identified with brand or company—for example, "I'm a Pepper"?

Commercial Characters

(D115) **Principal character(s) male:** The character(s) carrying the major on-camera role of delivering the commercial message is a male. Incidental, background on-camera appearance is not applicable.

(D116) **Principal character(s) female:** The character(s) carrying the major on-camera role of delivering the message is a female. Incidental, background on-camera appearance is not applicable.

(D117) **Principal character(s) child or infant:** The character carrying the major on-camera role of delivering the product message is a child or infant.

(D118)   **Principal character(s) racial or ethnic minority:** One or more of the principal on-camera characters is black, Hispanic, Oriental, or of some other clearly identifiable minority. Must be delivering a significant portion of message, not just cameo, background, or incidental appearance.

(D119)   **Principal character(s) celebrity:** The character(s) delivering the major portion of the message on camera is well known either by name or face. Celebrities may be athletes, movie stars, or well-known corporate figures (but not simply the identified head of a corporation).

(D120)   **Principal character(s) actor playing role of ordinary person:** Must be delivering the major portion of the message.

(D121)   **Principal character(s) real people:** Are one or more of the principal characters identified as real people (as opposed to actors playing a role)? This may take the form of a hidden camera or an interview.

(D122)   **Principal character(s) creation:** The principal character is a created role, person, or cartoon figure—for example, Ronald McDonald, Pillsbury Doughboy.

(D123)   **Principal character(s) animal:** Is one or more of the principal characters an animal (either real or animated)?

(D124)   **Principal character(s) animated:** Is one or more of the principal characters animated (cartoon figures)?

(D125)   **No principal character(s):** No central character or set of characters delivers a major portion of the commercial message, although there may be characters performing roles on camera relevant to the message.

(D126)   **Characters identified with company:** Is one or more of the characters in the commercial symbolic of or well identified with the company manufacturing and/or distributing the product? The character may be real, created, or animated but should be identified with the company, not a specific product—for example, Keebler Elves, Green Giant.

(D127)   **Background cast:** Are there people in the commercial other than the principal characters, people who serve as scenery or background—for example, people walking by, people sitting around a bar. These people are only incidental to the commercial message—that is, not active in making a product claim or demonstrating a product benefit.

(D128)   **Racial or ethnic minority character in minor role.**

(D129)   **Celebrity in minor role (cameo appearance).**

(D130)   **Animal(s) in minor role.**

(D131)   **Created character or cartoon characters in minor role.**

(D132)   **Real person in minor role (not professional actors):** May be actual consumers (specifically identified) or employees.

(D133)   **Recognized continuing character:** Is one or more of the principal or minor characters in the commercial recognized as a part of a continuing advertising campaign? Is the character associated with the product by virtue of previous appearances in commercials for the product?

(D134)   **Presenter/spokesperson on camera:** Is the audio portion of the commercial message delivered by voice-over announcer (person not on camera), character(s) on camera, or a combination of both? Codes: 1 = voice-over only, 2 = voice-over and on-camera characters, 3 = no voice-over, entire audio message delivered by on-camera characters.

Commercial Setting

(D135)   Is the commercial setting, or a significant part of it, indoors or in other humanmade structures (for example, a kitchen, garage, office, stadium, airplane)?

(D136)   Is the commercial setting, or a significant part of it, outdoors (mountains, rivers, backyard, garden, or other natural setting)? Do not include unnatural environments such as stadium or home driveway.

(D137)   There is no particular setting for the commercial; the setting is neutral, neither indoors nor outdoors.

Commercial Approach

(D138)   **Rational/emotional appeal:** A fairly straightforward presentation of the product's attributes and claims is a rational appeal. An emotional appeal does not appeal to reason but to feelings. Is the commercial primarily making a rational or an emotional appeal to the audience? Codes: 1 = more rational, 2 = balance of rational and emotional appeals, 3 = more emotional.

(D139)   **Positive or negative appeal:** A positive appeal to buy or use the product is based on what it will do for the consumer, the benefit offered, how the user will be better off. A negative appeal is based on what will happen to the consumer if he or she does not buy the product or what will not happen if the product is used (for example, wax floors won't yellow). Is the commercial making primarily a positive appeal (emphasis on how the product will help you, make you better, healthier) or negative appeal (emphasis on what will happen if you do not use the product, like cavities, or if you use competitor's product)? Codes: 1 = more negative, 2 = balance negative and positive, 3 = more positive.

(D140)   **Brand-differentiating message:** Is the principal message of the commercial unique to the product being advertised, or could any product make this claim? The commercial must make it clear that the message is unique; that is, the commercial must explicitly indicate the uniqueness or difference of the product. Dichotomous items are coded as follows: 1 = present, 0 = absent.

Created Variables

Research: Coded as present if any research is presented in the commercial—that is, if independent research (D014), company-sponsored research (D015), or unidentified research (D016) is present.

Total information: The sum of D001 to D026; the number of different pieces of information presented in the commercial.

Total propositions: The sum of D048 to D050; the number of different major appeals made in the commercial.

Total psychological appeals: The sum of D052 to D060; the number of different psychological appeals made in the commercial.

Total emotional content: The sum of D061 to D077; the number of emotions evoked by the commercial.

Timing and Counting Items and Product Category Identifiers

(X01)   **Type of commercial**
1. Animation
2. Storyboard on film
3. Live

(X02)   **Length of commercial (seconds)**

(X03)   **Times brand name mentioned (number)**

(X04)   **Time until product category identification (seconds)**

(X05)   **Time until brand name identified (spoken or written) (seconds)**

(X06)   **Time until product or package is shown (seconds)**

(X07)   **Time actual product is on screen (seconds)**

(X08)   **Time package is on screen (seconds)**

(X09)   **Times brand name or logo is shown on screen (number)**

(X10)   **Time brand name or logo is on screen (seconds)**

(X11)   **Principal message presented in first 10 seconds**

(X12)   **Number of vignettes**

(X13)   **Number of on-screen characters (0–9)**

(X14)   **Product category**

Food

11. Breakfast foods
12. Beverages
13. Primary and secondary courses (entrees, side dishes)
14. Snack foods
15. Other foods

Over-the-Counter Drugs

21. Remedies
22. Other

Household Products

31. Cleaners/Solvents/Sprays/Shiners
32. Other

Personal Care Products

41. Personal hygiene (shampoos, soaps, deodorants)
42. Other personal care products (grooming and beauty aids, cosmetics)
51. *Soft/hard goods, small durable and semidurable goods* (small appliances, mops, brooms)

Appendix B:
Items Failing to Obtain
Sufficient Reliability
in Initial Code Development

Items related to quality:

Production quality (within form)

Quality of product package camera shots

Quality of casting

Quality of music (how well played, recorded)

Quality of voices (easily understood, pleasant)

Quality of written script

Quality of video (use of color, movement, visual design, composition form or pattern)

Items related to believability:

Believability of claim (can product do what commercial says?)

Does commercial do a good job convincing the viewer that the product can do what the commercial promises?

Commercial leads to counterargument (does commercial suggest or otherwise cause viewer to raise negative arguments?)

Evaluative items:

Liking

Entertainment value

Confusion/clarity (was it easy or hard to follow the commercial message?)

Empathy with situation in commercial

Empathy with characters in commercial

Power of commercial to get and hold attention

Novelty of commercial (is this unusual for a product of this type?)

Congruence of commercial elements:

Do the spoken elements of the commercial go with the visual elements? Do the spoken and visual elements deliver the same message; that is, if you view the commercial with the sound off, would you get the same basic message as if delivered with the sound on?

Does the main character(s) reinforce something about the product by their role, occupation, or celebrity status presented in the commercial?

Does the principal character(s) in the commercial belong with the product? Does the character reinforce something about the product, a characteristic or benefit?

Is (are) the main character(s) in the commercial typical of intended users of this product by physical characteristics or age?

Key sales message versus execution dominance

Does the storyline/presentation/demonstration fit with the central product message?

Is the product integrated into the commercial execution?

Miscellaneous items:

Number of different sales points (number of benefits as opposed to supporting evidence)

Sales point is continuing claim

Sales point must be inferred from story line

Appendix C:
Univariate and Bivariate Statistics for All Variables

Table C–1
Univariate and Bivariate Statistics for All Variables

	Reliability[a]	Frequency[b]	Recall	Compre-hension	Persuasion
				Relationship to[c]	
Information content					
1. Price	.98	0.4	+ .08	+ .10	.00
2. Value	.98	2.0	+ .04	+ .04	− .01
3. Quality	.46	87.2	+ .01	− .03	.00
4. Economy/savings	.97	2.6	+ .07	+ .08	− .03
5. Dependability/reliability	.88	4.2	− .01	+ .04	− .05
6. Sensory (taste, smell)	.89	48.5	+ .09	− .03	+ .05
7. Aesthetic	.85	1.0	− .03	− .01	+ .05
8. Components/ingredients	.85	60.1	− .09	− .12	− .09
9. Availability	.99	3.2	− .06	− .05	+ .05
10. Packaging	1.00	1.9	− .05	− .06	− .02
11. Guarantees	1.00	0.4	− .01	− .04	− .03
12. Safety	.93	3.8	− .07	− .06	− .02
13. Nutrition/health	.86	27.6	− .24	− .18	− .14
14. Independent research	.95	0.7	− .02	− .04	+ .03
15. Company research	.98	0.1	− .04	− .02	− .07
16. Research (no source)	.93	2.0	− .07	− .06	− .01
Research findings (composite variables 14, 15, 16)	.94	2.8	− .08	− .08	− .01
17. New uses	.87	0.6	+ .04	.00	− .02
18. Company image/ reputation	.90	3.3	.00	− .02	− .07
19. Results of using	.78	55.2	− .01	+ .11	+ .04
20. User satisfaction	1.00	20.6	− .06	− .08	− .03

Table C–1 (continued)

	Reliability[a]	Frequency[b]	Relationship to[c]		
			Recall	Compre-hension	Persuasion
21. Superiority	.57	73.2	− .06	− .06	+ .04
22. Convenience of use	.87	7.9	+ .15	+ .21	+ .10
23. Special offer/event	1.0	0	N/A	N/A	N/A
24. New product or features	.96	47.3	− .05	− .01	+ .16
25. Use occasion	.91	0.7	− .00	+ .02	− .04
26. Characteristics/image of users	.86	1.6	− .03	− .05	− .01
Brand/product identification					
27. Nonproduct/multiproduct	.57		+ .02	+ .03	+ .16
28. Double-branded	.77	31.7	− .03	+ .05	+ .09
29. Manufacturer/distributor identification	.76	39.4	+ .01	+ .07	.00
30. Visual brand sign-off	.83	94.9	+ .07	+ .04	+ .03
31 Auditory sign-off	.86	70.8	+ .01	+ .02	− .02
Congruence of commercial elements					
32. Brand name reinforces	.77	27.0	+ .06	+ .08	+ .08
33. Setting not related	.81	2.4	+ .01	.00	− .05
34. Relevant setting	.66	6.9	− .03	− .07	− .04
35. Setting directly related	.86	64.7	+ .12	+ .11	+ .04
36. No setting	.93	20.6	− .09	− .07	+ .05
Visual devices					
37. Scenic beauty	.96	2.2	− .02	.00	− .08
38. Beauty of characters	.91	1.0	− .00	+ .03	− .04
39. Ugliness of characters	.98	0.1	− .04	− .02	− .02
40. Graphic displays	.92	6.5	− .08	− .07	− .04
41. Surrealistic visuals	.92	3.8	− .02	− .04	− .05
42. Substantive supers	.91	92.5	− .09	− .05	− .04
43. Visual tagline	.92	1.1	+ .02	+ .02	− .04
44. Visual memory device	.70	5.5	− .01	− .01	− .03
Auditory devices					
45. Memorable rhyme/mnemonic	.70	7.5	+ .15	+ .05	+ .03
46. Unusual sound effects	.83	1.8	+ .03	+ .02	− .03
47. Spoken tagline	.95	2.2	+ .05	+ .03	− .01
Promises, appeals, propositions					
48. Attributes/ingredients	.76	55.1	− .07	− .08	− .06
49. Product performance benefits	.84	67.7	− .06	+ .07	+ .01

	Reliability[a]	Frequency[b]	Relationship to[c]		
			Recall	Compre-hension	Persuasion
50. Psychological benefits	.59	1.2	+ .01	− .01	.00
51. Product reminder	.33	25.6	+ .07	− .03	− .08
52. Sexual appeal	.97	0.8	− .03	− .03	− .03
53. Comfort appeal	.83	0.6	− .03	.00	.00
54. Safety appeal	.93	1.2	− .03	− .04	− .08
55. Enjoying life	.80	10.2	+ .05	− .02	− .04
56. Welfare appeals	.90	0.3	.00	− .01	− .02
57. Social approval	.90	0.3	.00	− .01	− .02
58. Self-esteem	.89	3.0	.00	.00	+ .01
59. Achievement	1.00	0	N/A	N/A	N/A
60. Excitement/variety	.84	1.1	+ .06	+ .02	− .06
Commercial tone or atmosphere					
61. Cute/adorable	.93	7.7	+ .17	+ .04	− .01
62. Hard sell	.64	3.2	− .02	.00	+ .06
63. Warm/caring	.71	5.1	− .03	− .05	− .04
64. Modern/contemporary	.43	25.2	− .02	+ .03	+ .04
65. Wholesome/health	.55	6.9	− .07	− .04	− .04
66. Technological/futuristic	.94	1.9	− .05	− .06	− .02
67. Conservative/traditional	.68	20.1	− .10	− .05	− .06
68. Old fashioned/nostalgic	.93	0.6	.00	− .02	− .03
69. Happy/fun-loving	.82	4.8	+ .06	− .02	− .04
70. Cool/laid back	1.00	0.1	+ .01	+ .01	+ .01
71. Somber/serious	.59	5.8	− .05	− .01	.00
72. Uneasy/tense	.76	0.6	− .01	+ .02	+ .02
73. Relaxed/comfortable	.66	18.1	− .02	− .01	+ .08
74. Glamorous	.92	1.2	− .01	− .04	.00
75. Humorous	.85	5.3	+ .13	+ .07	+ .04
76. Suspenseful	.97	0.2	+ .01	.00	+ .02
77. Rough/rugged	.95	0.5	+ .09	+ .08	+ .08
Comparisons					
78. Direct comparison	.98	10.9	− .10	− .09	+ .01
79. Indirect comparison	.74	28.1	− .01	− .01	+ .07
80. Unsubstantiated claim (puffery)	.73	57.5	+ .09	+ .08	+ .04
Commercial structure					
81. Opening surprise/ suspense	.61	76.6	+ .10	+ .08	+ .06
82. Surprise in middle	.60	0.4	+ .04	+ .02	− .02
83. Surprise at closing	.87	0.1	− .02	− .02	− .01

Table C–1 (continued)

	Reliability[a]	Frequency[b]	Relationship to[c]		
			Recall	Compre-hension	Persuasion
84. Unusual setting/situation	.80	1.7	− .02	− .02	− .094
85. Humorous closing	.87	1.7	+ .01	+ .01	− .07
86. Blind lead-in	1.00	0.7	− .03	+ .01	− .01
Message in middle	.98	0.4	.00	− .01	+ .01
Commercial format					
88. Vignettes	.95	3.6	− .05	− .03	− .05
89. Continuity of action	.62	94.4	+ .06	+ .04	+ .07
90. Slife of life	.80	32.3	+ .04	+ .03	− .02
91. Testimonial of user	.82	13.5	− .05	− .02	− .06
92. Endorsement (celebrity/authority)	.96	3.7	− .02	− .02	− .04
93. Announcement	.78	2.6	− .08	− .04	+ .02
94. Demonstration (product use)	.74	59.7	+ .25	+ .17	+ .09
95. Demonstration (results)	.82	23.5	+ .09	+ .16	+ .06
96. Comedy/satire	.87	1.9	+ .08	+ .01	.00
97. Animation/cartoon[d]	1.00	6.7	+ .15	+ .05	+ .02
98. Stills/storyboard	.98	21.4	− .00	− .13	− .09
99. Moods/image dominant	.52	31.0	+ .03	+ .05	+ .05
100. Serious drama	.43	1.5	− .04	− .01	+ .03
101. Fantasy/surrealism	.89	5.2	+ .07	+ .01	.00
102. Problem/solution	.75	18.1	− .01	+ .06	+ .02
103. Interview	.98	1.5	− .05	− .02	− .03
104. Camera involves audience	.73	0.5	− .04	− .05	− .06
105. New wave/product graphics	.99	0.4	+ .01	+ .01	+ .09
106. Number of words	.94	2 = 0.3 3 = 99.7	—	—	—
107. Visual face	1.00	3 = 0.5 2 = 99.5	—	—	—
Music and dancing					
108. Music present	.96	42.3	.00	− .05	.00
109. Music major element	.97	11.5	+ .06	− .01	− .02
110. Music creates mood	.67	2.3	+ .02	− .02	− .05
111. Dancing	.99	0.5	.00	− .02	− .03
112. Music/dancing extravaganca	1.00	0.1	− .01	− .02	− .01
113. Well-known music	.99	0.9	+ .03	− .03	− .05
114. Continuing music theme	.97	2.0	+ .08	+ .06	+ .05

	Reliability[a]	Frequency[b]	Recall	Compre-hension	Persuasion
				Relationship to[c]	

Commercial characters

	Reliability[a]	Frequency[b]	Recall	Compre-hension	Persuasion
115. Male principal character	.96	53.9	− .06	− .11	− .10
116. Female principal character	.97	61.1	− .06	+ .02	− .03
117. Child/infant principal character	.99	12.7	+ .10	+ .05	+ .01
118. Racial/ethnic minority principal character	.99	1.3	+ .05	− .01	− .03
119. Celebrity principal character	.99	4.2	+ .02	.00	− .05
120. Actor playing role of principal character	.85	45.3	− .05	+ .02	+ .07
121. Real person principal character	.95	1.7	− .02	+ .01	− .02
122. Created principal character	.99	1.7	+ .02	− .03	− .06
123. Animal principal character	.99	8.4	+ .16	− .06	− .03
124. Animated cartoon principal character	1.00	12.5	+ .16	.04	− .01
125. No principal character	.93	6.3	− .07	+ .01	+ .07
126. Character identified with company	.95	0.7	+ .07	.00	− .07
127. Background cast	.92	26.8	− .03	− .08	− .12
128. Racial/ethnic minor role	.98	1.1	− .02	− .04	− .05
129. Celebrity in minor role	1.00	0	N/A	N/A	N/A
130. Animal(s) minor role	.96	1.8	+ .02	+ .02	+ .01
131. Created/cartoon minor character	.88	0.6	.00	− .01	− .01
132. Real person(s) minor role	.96	0.1	− .01	− .02	− .01
133. Continuing character in campaign	.96	0.6	+ .05	− .02	− .04
134. Spokesperson on camera	.64[c]	Voice over = 32.8 Voice over plus spokes-person = 60.0 Spokesperson = 7.2	− .02	− .06	− .03

Commercial setting

	Reliability[a]	Frequency[b]	Recall	Compre-hension	Persuasion
135. Indoors	.95	.63	+ .04	+ .08	+ .03
136. Outdoors	.97	22.6	+ .06	− .03	− .09
137. No setting	.93	22.9	− .11	− .09	+ .04

Table C–1 (continued)

	Reliability[a]	Frequency[b]	Relationship to[c]		
			Recall	Compre-hension	Persuasion
Commercial approach					
138. Emotional appeal	.37[c]	More rational = 28.4 Balanced = 64.0 More emotional = 7.5 More negative = .2	+.18	+.10	.06
139.	.29[c]	Balanced = 34.5 More positive = 65.2	+.04	−.04	−.10
140. Brand-differentiating message	.75	44.4	+.15	+.16	+.25
Timing and other variables					
V002. Length (seconds)	1.00	$\bar{x} = 30.4$ s.d. = 3.5	+.08	+.09	+.03
V003. Number of times brand name is mentioned	.95	$\bar{x} = 3.7$ s.d. = 1.7	+.09	+.02	+.02
V004. Time until product category identified	.87	$\bar{x} = 4.8$ s.d. = 4.2	−.08	−.02	−.04
V005. Time until brand name identified	.96	$\bar{x} = 6.2$ s.d. = 4.8	−.09	.00	−.01
V006. Time until product/package is shown	.94	$\bar{x} = 6.6$ s.d. = 5.1	−.08	−.03	−.04
V007. Time product is on screen (seconds)	.91	$\bar{x} = 17.3$ s.d. = 7.2	+.13	+.09	+.10
V008. Time package on screen (seconds)	.95	$\bar{x} = 13.6$ s.d. = 6.5	−.01	−.02	−.01
V009. Number of times brand name/logo is on screen	.84	$\bar{x} = 4.1$ s.d. = 2.3	+.07	−.03	+.01
V010. Time brand name/logo is on screen	.91	$\bar{x} = 14.6$ s.d. = 6.1	+.05	.00	−.01
V011. Principal message in first 10 seconds	.84	82.7%	+.05	−.01	+.03
V012. Vignettes	.78	$\bar{x} = .10$ s.d. = .55	−.02	+.01	−.05
V013. Number of on-screen characters	.97	$\bar{x} = 3.3$ s.d. = 2.8	.00	−.11	−.12
Created variables					
Total information (sum of variables 1 to 26)			−.13	−.09	+.01
Total proportions (sum of variables 48 to 51)			−.08	−.04	−.06
Total psychological appeals (sum of variables 52 to 60)			−.03	−.10	−.12
Total emotional appeals (sum of variables 53 to 77)			+.05	.00	+.01

	Reliability[a]	Frequency[b]	Recall	Compre-hension	Persuasion
				Relationship to[c]	
Commercial finish [nonlive (storyboard for example) = 27.8, live = 72.2]			+.13	+.12	+.07
Product categories (reliability = .99)					
Breakfast food	5.4				
Beverages	4.5		—	—	
Entrees	6.5				
Snacks	3.8	+		+	
All other food	18.6				
Over-the-counter remedies		14.7	—	—	—
All other over-the-counter products		10.0	—	—	
Cleansers/shiners/polishers		11.7			
All other household products		7.3	+	+	+
Hygiene products		4.4			
All other personal care		6.9	—	—	
Soft/hard goods		6.1	+	+	+

Notes: All statistical relationships are reported at two significance levels (.95 and .90) and for all variables regardless of their frequency of occurrence in the dataset. Two cautions should be observed in using the table:

1. For lower significance levels, the opportunity is great for pure statistical artifacts, or chance findings, to show up as being significant.

2. For variables occurring in only a few commercials, readers should not conclude that there is necessarily a relationship between that variable (for example, dancing in the commercial) and getting high recall or persuasion. The more appropriate interpretation is that a few specific commercials in which there happened to be dancing performed better than average. The results for variables that occurred in fewer than 50 commercials are better interpreted as idiosyncrasies of a small set of commercials rather than as a more general relationship between the presence of that element and performance of the commercial.

[a]The reliability statistic is a correlational measure of the degree to which the four coders (two coders for timing and counting variables) agree on each commercial for that variable. For nondichotomous categorical variables, a contingency coefficient is used (marked by a "c"). For the interval-scaled timing and counting variables, the reliability statistic is Pearson's R.

[b]Frequency is expressed as a percentage—0.4 = four-tenths of a percent of commercials had that characteristic; 2 = 2 percent; and so on. Since there were a total of 1,059 commercials in the database, each one-tenth percent is equivalent to roughly one commercial. $\bar{x}$ represents the mean and s.d. represents standard deviation.

[c]The statistics of relationship are all correlation measures between the (independent) commercial executional variable and the (dependent) commercial performance measures:

For the dichotomous variables: Eta

For the nondichotomous categorical variables: Eta

For the interval-scaled timing and counting variables and created variables (for example, total information): Pearson's R.

[d]Mainly driven by storyboard animatics, not animation in finished commercials; animation in finished commercials occurred in less than 1 percent of commercials.

Appendix D:
Frequency of
Individual Executional Variables
by Product Category

Table D–1
Frequency of Individual Executional Variables, by Product Category

Variable Codes[a]	Product Category Code												Total
	11	12	13	14	15	21	22	31	32	41	42	51	
D001[b]					0.1							0.3	0.4
D002		0.1			0.3	0.4	0.2		0.1		0.2	0.8	2.0
D003	4.2	4.3	6.8	3.1	17.0	13.6	7.2	10.5	6.4	3.4	5.6	5.0	87.2
D004					0.3	0.4	0.1	0.3	0.8	0.1	0.2	0.5	2.6
D005						1.3	0.3	0.4	0.8	0.2	0.3	0.9	4.2
D006	4.7	3.9	6.3	3.4	14.6	0.5	1.2	2.4	2.7	3.0	3.8	2.0	48.5
D007					0.1			0.1	0.3		0.1	0.4	1.0
D008	3.6	0.8	4.6	2.7	15.7	9.9	8.5	3.9	2.1	2.6	3.7	1.6	60.1
D009	0.1		0.4	0.1	0.7	0.6	0.5				0.4	1.1	3.2
D010		0.1	0.2		0.3	0.1	0.3		0.2		0.3		1.9
D011		0.1				0.1				0.2	0.1	0.1	0.4
D012						1.6	0.7	1.0	0.4				3.8
D013	3.2	0.4	1.3	1.5	7.4	5.0	7.5			0.5	0.6	0.1	27.6
D014		0.1			0.4		0.1				0.1		0.7
D015					0.1								0.1
D016	0.1	0.1			0.5	0.5	0.4	0.1			0.5		2.0
D017	0.1		0.2	0.1	0.1		0.1	0.1					0.6
D018		0.9	1.1	0.4		0.1	0.1	0.3				0.6	3.3
D019	0.2	0.6	0.7	0.4	3.8	12.7	4.4	12.8	5.8	2.7	6.1	4.8	55.2
D020	1.7	1.1	2.4	0.8	3.0	3.2	1.0	2.5	0.7	1.4	1.6	1.4	20.6
D021	3.1	2.9	3.9	2.2	14.2	13.3	6.8	9.7	5.0	3.7	4.8	3.4	73.6
D022	0.8	0.1	0.3	0.2	0.9	0.5		1.7	2.1	0.1	0.4	0.7	7.9
D023												0	

D024	1.8	0.8	1.8	2.2	7.4	7.2	5.8	7.9	4.1	3.1	3.8	1.1	47.3
D025		0.4					0.1	0.1				0.7	
D026				0.1	0.3	0.4	0.2			0.2	0.2	0.2	1.6
D027	/.2	/.1	/.5	/.2	/.1	/.1	/.2	/.4	/.2		/.3	/.2	0.2/2.2^c
D028	3.4	1.2	2.6	2.5	4.0	3.7	3.0	3.3	2.7	1.3	1.8	2.1	31.7
D029	5.1	2.4	5.5	3.2	5.6	5.3	2.5	2.8	1.8	0.6	1.0	3.1	39.4
D030	4.8	4.3	6.3	3.4	17.0	13.7	9.7	11.4	7.2	4.3	6.6	5.9	94.9
D031	2.6	4.0	4.5	3.0	12.9	9.1	7.8	8.5	5.7	2.9	5.0	4.4	70.8
D032													
—d	1.4	0.5	0.1	0.8	4.9	1.6	3.1	3.6	2.2	2.8	2.7	1.2	25.0
1.00	1.4	2.8	1.0	1.1	10.1	8.3	5.3	5.2	3.3	2.1	4.0	2.9	48.0
2.00	2.1	1.1	2.1	1.6	2.5	2.1	1.8	2.7	1.6	0.1	1.0	1.6	20.3
3.00	0.5	0.1	0.2	0.6	1.0	0.4	0.2	0.6	0.5	0.2	0.1	0.4	6.8
D033	0.2	0.1	0.3		1.1	0.3	0.2			0.1	0.1	0.1	2.4
D034	0.5	0.1	0.6	0.3	1.0	1.8	1.1	0.2		0.2	0.8	0.2	6.9
D035	4.2	3.3	4.5	2.4	10.7	7.5	3.7	11.1	7.3	2.4	3.2	4.2	64.7
D036	0.4	0.8	0.6	0.5	4.6	3.7	3.8	1.1	0.5	0.9	2.3	1.5	20.6
D037		0.3	0.1	0.1	0.9	0.2	0.3	0.1			0.2	0.1	2.2
D038	0.1		0.1	0.1	0.2						0.2	0.3	1.0
D039						0.1							0.1
D040					0.1	2.6	1.0	0.2	0.5	0.6	1.0	0.5	6.5
D041			0.2		0.6	1.1	0.4	0.6	0.3	0.1	0.3	0.3	3.8
D042	4.2	4.3	5.5	2.9	16.8	14.2	9.6	11.0	6.6	4.5	6.8	5.8	92.5
D043		0.1				0.3	0.4	0.1	0.1	0.1			1.1
D044	0.1	0.2	0.3		0.8	1.7	0.8	0.8	0.3		0.2	0.2	5.5
D045	5.3	3.3	3.8	3.7	17.4	14.8	10.2	10.9	0.6	0.1	0.1	0.9	7.5
D046					0.3	0.5	0.1	0.5	0.1			0.2	1.8
D047		0.1		0.1	0.2	0.7	0.4	0.3	0.3	0.1	0.1	0.1	2.2

Table D–1 (continued)

Variable Codes[a]	Product Category Code												
	11	12	13	14	15	21	22	31	32	41	42	51	Total
D048	3.8	1.0	5.1	3.0	14.5	9.1	7.7	2.6	1.8	2.4	2.7	1.3	55.1
D049	2.1	0.4	0.6	0.3	5.1	15.4	6.6	13.1	7.6	4.2	6.7	5.3	67.7
D050		0.3		0.1	0.2	0.1					0.1	0.4	1.2
D051	2.8	3.4	3.9	1.0	4.8	1.6	1.7	1.7	1.0	0.8	1.6	1.3	25.6
D052		0.2	0.1		0.1					0.1	0.2	0.1	0.8
D053										0.2	0.1	0.3	0.6
D054						0.6	0.2		0.3		0.1		1.2
D055	0.5	0.34	2.6	0.8	2.7							0.2	10.2
D056						0.1		0.1	0.1				0.3
D057		0.3											0.3
D058	0.1		0.1	0.3	0.3		0.7			0.2	0.7	0.7	3.0
D059													0.0
D060		0.5	0.1		0.2							0.3	1.1
D061	0.7	0.3	1.9	0.2	3.2	0.1	0.1	0.3	0.5		0.1	0.4	7.7
D062	0.2				0.1	0.5	0.9	0.4	0.2		0.1	0.8	3.2
D063	0.1	0.8	0.5	0.1	1.6	0.7	0.3			0.1	0.5	0.3	5.1
D064	0.5	0.7	1.6	0.6	3.2	3.6	1.9	3.9	2.1	1.3	2.6	2.8	25.2
D065	1.5		1.6	0.8	1.5	0.4	0.7			0.1	0.3		6.9
D066	0.1		0.5		0.5	0.8	0.3	0.1				0.2	1.9
D067	1.0	0.9	0.5	0.6	2.1	4.3	2.7	2.6	1.7	1.4	1.7	0.5	20.1
D068		0.1	0.3			0.1			0.1				0.6
D069	0.3	0.7	1.3	0.1	1.2		0.3	0.1	0.2	0.2	0.1	0.3	4.8
D070												0.1	0.1
D071	0.1	0.1			0.2	2.8	1.6	0.1	0.3	0.1	0.2	0.3	5.8

D072	1.0						0.5			0.1	1.7		0.6
D073	0.6	1.6	0.8	0.9	4.1	1.5	1.0	2.3	1.1	1.5	0.6	0.5	18.1
D074	0.3	0.2	1.4	0.1	0.1	0.4		0.3	0.2	0.1		0.2	1.2
D075		0.3		0.5	1.0		0.1					0.4	5.3
D076					0.1							0.1	0.2
D077		0.1			0.1					0.2	0.7	0.1	0.5
D078	1.2	0.3	0.2	0.1	1.2	4.0	1.6	0.4	0.5	1.2	1.8	0.5	10.9
D079	2.2	0.9	1.3	1.1	4.6	4.7	2.6	5.0	2.2	1.3	4.6	1.4	28.1
D080	3.4	2.9	4.8	2.2	11.3	8.3	4.0	7.6	3.5	2.0	4.6	3.9	57.5
D081	0.1	2.6	4.9	3.1	15.2	11.0	8.1	9.0	6.0	2.6	0.1	5.6	76.6
D082		0.1	0.1										0.4
D083			0.1										0.1
D084		0.2	0.1		0.7	0.2	0.1	0.1			0.1	0.2	1.7
D085			0.2		0.4	0.5		0.2	0.1			0.1	1.7
D086					0.3	0.3						0.1	0.7
D087					0.2		0.1					0.1	0.4
D088	0.2	0.1	0.5		0.1	1.0	0.6	0.5	0.3	0.2	0.3	0.1	3.6
D089	5.6	4.3	6.2	4.0	17.3	13.1	9.3	11.1	7.3	4.3	6.0	5.9	94.4
D090	3.4	2.1	3.3	1.3	5.5	4.2	2.2	3.0	2.2	1.8	1.1	2.0	32.3
D091	0.7	0.2	0.9	0.6	1.5	2.1	1.2	2.2	0.7	1.0	1.3	1.0	13.5
D092	0.1	0.1			1.0	1.1	0.8	0.1	0.1	0.1	0.1	0.3	3.7
D093		0.1			0.2	0.6	1.3	0.1	0.2		0.1	0.1	2.6
D094	4.9	3.4	5.3	2.0	12.8	3.3	1.4	9.4	6.7	1.2	4.2	4.9	59.7
D095	0.1			0.2	1.0	4.7	0.9	9.6	3.2	0.8	1.1	1.8	23.5
D096	0.2	0.4	0.3		0.7	0.1	0.2	0.2				0.2	1.9
D097			0.4	0.8	2.1	0.3	0.6	0.6	0.9	0.1	0.5	0.1	6.7
D098	1.0	1.2	1.1	0.5	7.0	0.7	2.4	2.7	1.8	0.7	1.7	0.5	21.4
D099	1.6	3.2	2.5	1.5	5.9	3.4	2.7	3.3	0.8	1.2	2.7	2.1	31.0

Table D–1 (continued)

Variable Codes[a]	Product Category Code												
	11	12	13	14	15	21	22	31	32	41	42	51	Total
D100		0.1				0.4	0.4	0.1	0.2	0.1	0.1	0.1	1.5
D101	0.2	0.1	0.4	0.2	1.4	0.7	0.4	0.8	0.6		0.2	0.3	5.2
D102	0.1	0.1		0.1	0.3	5.4	1.0	6.1	2.1	0.8	1.1	0.9	18.1
D103			0.2	0.1	0.3	0.4	0.3			0.1	0.2		1.5
D104			0.1		0.1	0.2	0.1						0.5
D105	0.1		0.1						0.1			0.1	0.4
D106	0.1												0.1
D107	0.1		0.1		(All others code = 2.00)				0.3	0.1	0.1	0.1	0.5
D108	2.0	3.3	4.8	1.6	9.2 (All others code = 2.00)	3.7	2.5	3.6	2.7	1.9	3.8	3.3	42.3
D109	1.4	1.0	2.4	0.6	3.0	0.1	0.2	0.6	0.8	0.4	0.4	0.6	11.5
D110		0.4	0.1	0.1	0.6	0.3	0.2	0.1				0.5	2.3
D111		0.1	0.1		0.1				0.1			0.1	0.5
D112	0.1												0.1
D113	0.1	0.1	0.1		0.2			0.2	0.2	0.1			0.9
D114	0.1		1.4	0.2	0.1							0.2	2.0
D115	4.0	4.0	4.7	2.8	8.7	11.2	5.6	3.3	2.5	1.3	2.9	2.8	53.9
D116	3.0	1.7	3.7	2.8	7.8	9.5	4.9	8.9	5.6	4.2	5.5	3.4	61.1
D117	2.9	0.3	2.5	1.2	1.5	0.4	1.4	1.2	0.6	0.2	0.3	0.4	12.7
D118		0.2	0.5		0.1		0.1	0.1	0.2		0.1	0.1	1.3
D119	0.2		0.4		0.7	1.2	1.0		0.1		0.3	0.5	4.2
D120	2.7	1.9	2.6	2.0	5.2	8.4	4.5	5.7	3.3	3.4	3.2	2.4	45.3
D121	0.1		0.2	0.1	0.2	0.2	0.3	0.2	0.3		0.2		1.7
D122	0.3	0.4		0.4	0.2				0.2	0.2		0.1	1.7

D123		0.1	0.1		7.6	0.1	0.2	0.1	0.1		0.1	0.1	8.4
D124	0.3	0.7	0.5	1.3	4.8	0.6	1.0	0.7	1.7		0.6	0.1	12.5
D125	0.3	0.5	0.2	0.1	0.7	0.6	1.5	1.2	0.5		0.2	0.7	6.3
D126		0.3		0.2	0.2					0.3			0.7
D127	1.6	2.7	2.6	0.9	4.8	3.4	2.8	1.6	0.9		1.8	2.8	26.8
D128	0.1	0.2	0.6			0.1				0.8		0.2	1.1
D129					Code = 0 only								
D130	0.2	0.1	0.2	0.1	1.0	0.2		0.1	0.2				1.8
D131		0.1	0.1	0.2					0.1				0.6
D132													0.1
D133		0.2		0.2	0.1	0.1						0.1	0.6
D134													
1.00	1.3	2.3	1.3	0.6	9.3	2.0	3.9	3.7	2.6	1.0	2.0	2.5	32.4
2.00	4.0	1.9	5.4	3.1	7.7	12.4	5.1	7.3	3.8	3.6	4.1	3.4	62.0
3.00	0.2	0.1	0.2		0.7	1.1	0.9	0.7	0.5	0.1	0.4	0.5	5.6
D135	3.7	2.1	3.9	1.8	8.1	9.5	4.9	10.7	7.1	3.4	4.0	3.4	63.0
D136	1.9	1.8	2.5	1.7	6.5	2.1	1.7	0.7	0.3	0.5	1.2	1.9	22.6
D137	0.5	0.9	1.0	0.7	5.2	4.1	4.0	1.0	0.5	0.9	2.5	1.9	22.9
D138													
1.00	1.1	0.2	0.4	0.4	1.7	4.9	4.1	3.3	2.7	0.9	1.4	1.1	22.3
2.00	2.7	2.0	3.2	2.4	11.3	7.4	4.1	6.0	2.6	2.1	3.2	3.1	50.2
3.00	0.3	1.2	0.9	0.4	2.2				0.1		0.3	0.4	5.8
D139													
1.00						0.1	0.1	0.1					0.2
2.00	0.8	0.5	0.8	1.1	4.6	5.3	2.4	5.5	1.7	1.6	2.0	0.8	27.0
3.00	3.7	3.5	5.6	2.0	9.2	6.4	5.3	3.6	3.3	1.7	3.7	3.0	50.9
X01													
1.00	0.1	0.3	0.2	0.7	3.0	0.4	0.6	1.2	0.9	0.1	0.6	0.1	8.1

Table D–1 (continued)

Variable Codes[a]	Product Category Code												Total
	11	12	13	14	15	21	22	31	32	41	42	51	
2.00	0.9	1.1	0.8	0.8	5.5	1.0	2.4	2.3	1.9	0.6	1.6	0.5	19.6
3.00	4.3	3.1	5.5	2.3	10.0	13.2	7.1	8.2	4.4	3.8	4.7	5.5	72.2
X11													
Yes	3.6	3.3	4.9	3.1	15.0	9.6	6.7	8.8	6.7	3.1	4.9	5.0	75.0
No	1.1	0.7	0.8	0.4	2.5	2.9	2.0	1.9	0.3	1.0	1.2	0.8	15.7

[a]See appendix A for descriptions of variables.

[b]Read 0.1 percent of all 1,059 commercials had variables D001 and were in the "other food" product category. Variable D001 occurred in a total of 0.4 percent of all commercials overall; that is, four commercials had information on price.

[c]For code 27, upper half is 1.00; lower half is 3.00; all others are 2.00.

[d]Missing data.

Appendix E:
ARS Sampling Procedures

Sample Size Policy

As most of you know, Research Systems is committed to the principles of sound measurement:

> The measurement results generated from each RSC system will meet the following standards of soundness before and as long as they are marketed:
>
> 1. The degree of reliability will be known, and the limits fully reported in the course of every sales effort and with all data results.
> 2. The limits of reliability will be such that the data as priced is a reasonable value.
> 3. Validation will be sought and reported without exclusion.[a]

The ARS measurement system was designed to generate Persuasion samples of 200–300 respondents, and Recall samples of 150–200 respondents, in order to meet the reliability (and discrimination) standards covered by the second statement above.

While most clients recognize the importance of adequate samples, we find that in some instances the subgroups reported are so small that inferences drawn from the data may be misleading.

We have debated this sample size issue now for several years and, in order to meet the requirements of sound measurement, have decided on the following policy:

> ARS will generate data from Persuasion samples of no less than 100 respondents.
>
> This will also ensure that Related Recall samples are adequate in size.

From Research Systems Corporation, *Basic Research Notes.*
[a]"Research Systems Corporation Operation Philosophy and Goals," 1970, p. 5.

Defining ARS Analytical Samples and Critical Cells

The ARS methodology is based on random samples, as opposed to quota or prerecruited samples, so ARS respondents are not pre-alerted or pre-conditioned to the purpose of the test.

The measures are administered to a random sampling of men and women. The specific "Analytical Sample," "Critical Cell," and other subgroups for each commercial test are defined according to the following considerations.

1. The recommended "Analytical Sample" is comprised of anyone who *could* purchase/use the product being advertised.

2. The recommended "Critical Cell" is comprised of anyone who *does* normally make purchases in the category as shown in the Persuasion photograph. If both are defined properly, the Critical Cell is always a subset of the Analytical Sample.

3. Questions used to identify relevant sub-samples should be clear and concise.

4. The smaller the sample size, the less meaningful the results. Persuasion sub-samples of under 100 respondents will not be shown in ARS reports.

5. The usage questioning sequence is administered *after* exposure to the programs with commercials, so the more effective the advertising, the more likely respondents are to be favorable towards the test brand. If a question asks for favorite brand or brand most often used, respondents will be inclined to give the "right" answer.

6. The more detailed the usage questioning, the more likely the playback of that detail in the Recall Measure.

7. When asked, we generally recommend that the measurement results be looked at among Total Analytical Sample and the Critical Cell only. This generally required a simple question regarding purchasing or usage in the product category.

References

Achenbaum, A.A. 1972. "Advertising Doesn't Manipulate Consumers." *Journal of Advertising Research* 2:3–13.

Anderson, Norman H. 1981. "Integration Theory Applied to Cognitive Responses and Attitudes." In R.E. Petty, T.M. Ostrom, and T.C. Brock, eds., *Cognitive Responses in Persuasion.* Hillsdale, N.J.: Lawrence Erlbaum Associates.

Assael, H., J.H. Kofron, and W. Burg. 1967. "Advertising Performance as a Function of Print Ad Characteristics." *Journal of Advertising Research* 7:20–26.

Bauer, Raymond A., and Stephen A. Greyser. 1968. *Advertising in America: The Consumer View.* Boston: Harvard University.

Belch, G.E. 1981. "An Examination of Comparative and Noncomparative Television Commercials: The Effects of Claim Variation and Repetition on Cognitive Response and Message Acceptance." *Journal of Marketing Research* 18: 333–349.

Borden, Neil H. 1942. *The Economic Effects of Advertising.* Homewood, Ill.: Richard D. Irwin.

Burke Marketing Research, Inc. 1978. *The Effect of Environmental and Executional Variables on Overall Memorability.* Cincinnati: Burke Marketing Research.

Calder, B.J., and B. Sternthal. 1980. "Television Commercial Wearout: An Information Processing View." *Journal of Marketing Research* 17:173–186.

Calder, B.J., L.W. Phillips, and A.M. Tybout. 1981. "Designing Research for Application." *Journal of Consumer Research* 8:197–207.

Caples, J. 1933. *Tested Advertising Methods.* New York: Harper and Brothers.

Diamond, Daniel S. 1968. "A Quantitative Approach to Magazine Advertisement Format Selection." *Journal of Marketing Research* 5:376–387.

Estes, W.K. 1980. "Comments on Directions and Limitations of Current Efforts Toward Theories of Decision Making." In T.S. Wallsten, ed. *Cognitive Processes in Choice and Decision Behavior.* Hillsdale, N.J.: Lawrence Erlbaum Associates.

Fishbein, Martin, and Icek Ajzen. 1981. "Acceptance, Yielding, and Impact: Cognitive Processes in Persuasion." In R.E. Petty, T.M. Ostrom, and T.C. Brock, eds. *Cognitive Responses in Persuasion.* Hillsdale, N.J.: Lawrence Erlbaum Associates.

Gibson, Lawrence D. 1983. "Not Recall." *Journal of Advertising Research* 23:39–46.

Gorn, G.J. 1982. "The Effects of Music in Advertising on Choice Behavior: A Classical Conditioning Approach." *Journal of Marketing* 46:94–101.

Greenwald, A.G. 1968. "Cognitive Learning, Cognitive Response to Persuasion and Attitude Change." In A.G. Greenwald, T.C. Brock, and T.M. Ostrom, eds. *Psychological Foundations of Attitudes.* New York: Academic Press.

Hendon, D.W. 1973. "How Mechanical Factors Affect Ad Perception." *Journal of Advertising Research* 13:39–45.

Higgens, Denis, ed. 1965. *The Art of Writing Advertising.* Chicago: Crain Books.

Holbrook, Morris B., and Donald R. Lehmann. 1980. "Form vs. Content in Predicting Starch Scores." *Journal of Advertising Research* 20:53–62.

Holley, J.W., and J.P. Guilford. 1964. "A Note on the G Index of Agreement." *Educational and Psychological Measurement* 24:749–754.

Holman, Rebecca H., and Sid Hecker. 1983. "Advertising Impact: Creative Elements Affecting Brand Saliency." *Current Issues and Research in Advertising* 6: 157–172.

Hovland, C.I., I.L. Janis, and H.H. Kelly. 1953. *Communication and Persuasion.* New Haven: Yale University Press.

Jacoby, Jacob, Robert W. Chestnut, and William Silberman. 1977. "Consumer Use and Comprehension of Nutrition Information." *Journal of Consumer Research* 4:119–128.

Johnsen, Thore H. 1976. *Advertising, Market Equilibrium, and Information.* Ph.D. dissertation, Carnegie-Mellon University.

Kihlstrom, Richard E., and Michael H. Riordan. 1984. "Advertising as a Signal." *Journal of Political Economy* 92:427–450.

Klein, Benjamin, and Keith B. Leffler. 1981. "The Role of Market Forces in Assuring Contractural Performance." *Journal of Political Economy* 89:615–641.

Kotler, Philip, and Gary L. Lilien. 1983. *Marketing Decision Making: A Model Building Approach.* New York: Harper & Row.

Kuhn, Thomas. 1970. *The Structure of Scientific Revolutions,* 2nd ed. Chicago: University of Chicago Press.

Lavidge, R., and G.A. Steiner. 1961. "A Model for Predictive Measurements of Advertising Effectiveness." *Journal of Marketing* 24:59–62.

Lingle, John J., and Thomas H. Ostrom. 1981. "Principles of Memory and Cognition in Attitude Formation." In R.E. Petty, T.M. Ostrom, and T.C. Brock, eds. *Cognitive Responses in Persuasion.* Hillsdale, N.J.: Lawrence Erlbaum Associates.

Lutz, Richard J., and John L. Swasy. 1977. "Integrating Cognitive Structure and Cognitive Response Approaches for Monitoring Communication Effects." In William D. Perreault, ed. *Advances in Consumer Research,* 4, Atlanta Ga.: Association for Consumer Research.

McCollum/Spielman/and Company, Inc. 1976. *The Influence of Executional Elements on Commercial Effectiveness.* Great Neck, N.Y.: McCollum/Spielman/and Company, Inc.

McEwen, J., and C. Leavitt. 1976. "A Way to Describe TV Commercials." *Journal of Advertising Research* 16:35–39.

McGrath, Joseph E., and David Brinberg. 1983. "External Validity and the Research Process: A Comment on the Calder/Lynch Dialogue." *Journal of Consumer Research* 10:115–124.

Moore, J. 1982. Mapes and Ross, personal communication.

Moriarty, Sandra Ernst. 1983. "Beyond the Hierarchy of Effects: A Conceptual Framework." *Current Issues and Research in Advertising* 6:45–55.

Nelson, Phillip. 1970. "Information and Consumer Behavior." *Journal of Political Economy* 78:311–329.

———. 1974. "Advertising as Information." *Journal of Political Economy* 82: 729–754.

———. 1978. "Advertising as Information Once More." In David G. Tuerck, ed. *Issues in Advertising: The Economics of Persuasion.* Washington, D.C.: American Enterprise Institute.

Ogilvy, D. 1964. *Confessions of an Advertising Man.* New York: Atheneum.

———, and J. Raphaelson. 1982. "Research on Advertising Techniques that Work—and Don't Work." *Harvard Business Review,* July–August, pp. 14–16.

Olson, Jerry C., D.R. Toy, and P.A. Dover. 1982. "Do Cognitive Responses Mediate the Effects of Advertising Content on Cognitive Structure." *Journal of Consumer Research* 9:245–262.

Osgood, C.E., C.J. Suci, and P.H. Tannenbaum. 1957. *The Measurement of Meaning.* Urbanna: University of Illinois Press.

Palda, Kristian S. 1966. "The Hypothesis of a Hierarchy of Effects: A Partial Evaluation." *Journal of Marketing Research* 3:13–24.

Percy, Larry. 1983. "A Review of the Effect of Specific Advertising Elements upon Overall Communication Response." *Current Issues and Research in Advertising* 6:77–118.

———, and John R. Rossiter. 1980. *Advertising Strategy: A Communication Theory Approach.* New York: Praeger.

Petty, R.E. 1977a. "The Importance of Cognitive Responses in Persuasion." In W.D. Perreault, ed. *Advances in Consumer Research, Vol. 4,* Atlanta, Ga.: Association for Consumer Research.

———. 1977b. *A Cognitive Response Analysis of the Temporal Persistence of Attitude Changes Induced by Persuasive Communications.* Ph.D. dissertation, Ohio State University.

———, and J.T. Cacioppo. 1980. "Effects of Issue Involvement on Attitudes in an Advertising Context." In J.G. Gorn and M.E. Goldberg, eds. *Proceedings of the Division 23 Program.* Annual Convention of the American Psychological Association, Montreal, Canada.

———, Thomas M. Ostrom, and Timothy C. Brock, eds. 1981. *Cognitive Responses in Persuasion.* Hillsdale, N.J.: Lawrence Erlbaum Associates, Inc.

Radio Recall Research, Inc. 1981. "Characteristics Leading to Significant Differences in Recall Rates." Holmdel, N.J.: Radio Recall Research, Inc.

Raj, S.P. 1982. "The Effects of Advertising on High and Low Loyalty Consumer Segments." *Journal of Consumer Research* 9:77–89.

Ramond, Charles. 1976. *Advertising Research: The State of the Art.* New York: Association of National Advertisers.

Ray, Michael L. 1973. *Marketing Communication and the Hierarchy-of-Effects.* Cambridge, Mass.: Marketing Science Institute.

———. 1975. "Microtheoretical Notions of Behavioral Science and the Problems of Advertising," Report No. 75-101. Cambridge, Mass.: Marketing Science Institute.

———. 1982. *Advertising and Communication Management.* Englewood Cliffs, N.J.: Prentice-Hall.

Reeves, Rosser. 1961. *Reality in Advertising,* New York: Alfred A. Knopf.

Research Systems Corporation. 1982. *The Reliability of the ARS Persuasion and Recall Measures, 1981 Data.* Evansville, In.: Research Systems Corporation.

———. 1983a. *Advertising Caused Awareness and Trial, ARS Predictive Validity for New Brand Advertising.* Evansville, In.: Research Systems Corporation.

———. 1983b. *Advertising Quality and Sales, ARS Predict Validity for Established Brand Advertising.* Evansville, In.: Research Systems Corporation.

———. 1984. *Understanding Fair Share Persuasion.* Evansville, In.: Research Systems Corporation.

Resnik, Alan, and Bruce L. Stern. 1977. "An Analysis of Information Content in Television Advertising." *Journal of Marketing* 41:50–53.

Ross, Harold L., Jr. 1982. "Recall Versus Persuasion: An Answer." *Journal of Advertising Research* 22:13–16.

Rossiter, John R. 1981. "Predicting Starch Scores." *Journal of Advertising Research* 21:63–68.

———, and Percy, Larry. 1983. "Visual Communications in Advertising." In Richard Jackson Harris, ed. *Information Processing in Advertising.* Hillsdale, N.J.: Lawrence Erlbaum Associates.

Scott, Walter Dill. 1903. *The Theory of Advertising.* Boston: Small, Maynard and Company.

———. 1908a. *The Psychology of Advertising.* Boston: Small, Maynard and Company.

———. 1908b. *The Psychology of Advertising in Theory and Practice.* Boston: Small, Maynard and Company.

Shanteau, James. 1983. "Cognitive Psychology Looks at Advertising: Commentary on a Hobbit's Adventure." In Richard Jackson Harris, ed. *Information Processing Research in Advertising.* Hillsdale, N.J.: Lawrence Erlbaum Associates.

Sherif, M., and H. Cantril. 1945. "The Psychology of Attitudes: I." *Psychological Review* 52:295–319.

———. 1946. "The Psychology of Attitudes: II." *Psychological Review* 53:1–24.

Shimp, T.A., and L.G. Gresham. 1983. "An Information Processing Perspective on Recent Advertising Literature." *Current Issues and Research in Advertising* 6:39–75.

Silk, Alvin J., and Glen L. Urban. 1978. "Pre-Test Market Evaluation of New Packaged Goods: A Model and Measurement Methodology." *Journal of Marketing Research* 15:171–191.

Starch, D. (1923. *Principles of Advertising.* Chicago: A.W. Shaw Co.

Sternthal, B., and C.S. Craig. 1973. "Humor in Advertising." *Journal of Marketing* 37:12–18.

Stewart, D.W., and Michael J. Haley. 1983. "A Theory of Marketing Dominance." Working Paper No. 83-116. Nashville, Tenn.: Owen Graduate School of Management, Vanderbilt University.

Stewart, D.W., D.H. Furse, and R. Kozak. 1983. "A Guide to Commercial Copytesting Services." *Current Issues and Research in Advertising* 6:1–44.

Stewart, D.W., C. Pechmann, S. Ratneshwar, J. Stroud, and B. Bryant. 1985a. "Advertising Evaluation: A Review of Measures." *Proceedings of the Winter Educators' Conference of the American Marketing Association.* (forthcoming).

————. 1985b. "Methodological and Theoretical Foundations of Advertising Copy Testing: A Review." In *Current Issues and Research in Advertising.* (forthcoming).

Strong, E.K. 1912. "The Effect of Length of Series upon Recognition." *Psychological Review* 19:44–47.

————. 1916. "The Factors Affecting a Permanent Impression Developed through Repetition." *Journal of Experimental Psychology* 1:319–338.

————. 1925. *The Psychology of Selling.* New York: McGraw-Hill.

Twedt, Dik W. 1952. "A Multiple Factor Analysis of Advertising Readership." *Journal of Applied Psychology* 37:207–215.

Valiente, R. 1973. "Mechanical Correlates of Ad Recognition." *Journal of Advertising Research* 13:13–18.

White, P. 1927. *Advertising Research.* New York: D. Appleton and Co.

Wolinsky, Archer. 1981. "Prices as Signals of Product Quality." Economic Discussion Paper No. 232. Murray Hill, N.J.: Bell Laboratories.

————. 1983. "Prices as Signals of Product Quality." *Review of Economic Studies* 50: 647–658.

Wright, Peter L. 1973. "The Cognitive Processes Mediating Acceptance of Advertising." *Journal of Marketing Research* 10:53–62.

————. 1981. "Cognitive Responses to Mass Media Advocacy." In R.E. Petty, T.M. Ostrom, and T.C. Brock, eds. *Cognitive Responses in Persuasion.* Hillsdale, N.J.: Lawrence Erlbaum Associates.

————, and F. Barbour. 1977. "Phased Decision Strategies: Sequels to an Initial Screening." In *North Holland/TIMS Studies in Management Sciences: Multiple Criteria Decision Making,* vol. 6. Amsterdam: North Holland, pp. 91–109.

Zeleny, M. 1982. *Multiple Criterion Decision Making.* New York: McGraw-Hill.

Zielske, Ho. 1982. "Does Day-After Recall Penalize Feeling Ads." *Journal of Advertising Research* 22:19–22.

Index

About the Authors

David W. Stewart is associate dean and an associate professor of marketing at the Owen Graduate School of Management, Vanderbilt University, where he has been since 1980. Prior to joining the faculty at the Owen School, he was an associate professor of psychology and business at Jacksonville State University. He also served as a research manager with Needham, Harper, and Steers Advertising, Chicago, and a research psychologist with the state of Louisiana. Dr. Stewart received his B.A. (1972) from Northeast Louisiana University and his M.A. (1973) and Ph.D. (1974) in psychology from Baylor University. He is a member of Phi Kappa Phi, Beta Gamma Sigma, and Alpha Iota Delta honoraries, a fellow of the American Psychological Association, and president of the Division of Consumer Psychology of the American Psychological Association. Dr. Stewart's interests include consumer behavior, marketing research methods, advertising evaluation, decision making, and marketing strategy. His published work has appeared in the *Journal of Marketing, Journal of Marketing Research, Journal of Consumer Research, Journal of Advertising Research, Journal of Applied Psychology, Current Issues and Research in Advertising, Journal of the Academy of Management,* and numerous other publications on business, marketing, and psychology. He has also authored a book, *Secondary Research,* published by Sage Publications. In addition, he has consulted with numerous firms on a wide range of marketing problems. Dr. Stewart is a native of Baton Rouge, Louisiana. He and his wife, Lenora, and their two children, Sarah, 6, and Rachel, 2, have lived in Nashville for 5 years.

David. H. Furse is president and founder of the Nashville Consulting Group, Inc., a general business consulting firm emphasizing marketing research and planning. He received his B.A. from the University of Georgia in 1965 and his M.A. from the University of Illinois in 1967. After serving for 2 years as an infantry lieutenant at the U.S. Army Special Warfare School at Ft. Bragg, North Carolina, and in Vietnam, he received his Ph.D. in business administration from Georgia State University in 1974. Dr. Furse taught at Vanderbilt

University's Owen Graduate School of Management for 6 years and at Michigan State University for 5 years before starting the Nashville Consulting Group. He has consulted for over 10 years with major banks, manufacturers, retailers, mass media, and start-up firms as an expert in marketing and advertising research. His published research has appeared in the *Journal of Marketing Research, Journal of Advertising Research, Journal of Consumer Research, Journal of Advertising,* and *Psychology and Marketing.* He has received numerous research grants and awards for his work in advertising research, consumer information processing, and survey research methods. Dr. Furse conducts executive seminars in the United States and abroad on strategic market planning and on advertising strategy and evaluation. Dr. Furse is a native of Atlanta, Georgia. He and his wife, Gunn, of Stockholm, Sweden, and their two children, Kristina, 11, and Erik, 9, have lived in Nashville for 8 years.